Unto Death

By the Author

The Same Sea

Israel, Palestine and Peace

Fima

To Know a Woman

The Slopes of Lebanon

Black Box

A Perfect Peace

In the Land of Israel

Where the Jackals Howl

The Hill of Evil Counsel

Soumchi

Touch the Water, Touch the Wind

Elsewhere Perhaps

My Michael

Amos Oz

UNTO DEATH

TWO NOVELLAS
CRUSADE & LATE LOVE

TRANSLATED BY

Nicholas de Lange
in collaboration with the Author

The Toby Press

The Toby Press LLC
POB 8531, New Milford, CT. 06676-8531, USA
& POB 2455, London WIA 5WY, England
www.tobypress.com

The translation of *Crusade* first appeared in *Commentary*

ISBN 1 59264 037 0, *paperback*

A CIP catalogue record for this title
is available from the British Library

Typeset in Garamond by Jerusalem Typesetting

Printed and bound in the United States by
Thomson-Shore Inc., Michigan

In memory of my father
Yehuda Arieh Klausner

Contents

Crusade

Chapter one

I t all began with outbreaks of discontent in the villages.

Day by day bad omens began to appear in the poorer areas. An old farmer of Galland saw the form of a fiery chariot in the sky. In Sareaux an ignorant old woman croaked out oracles couched in the purest Latin. Rumors went around of a cross in an out-of-the-way church which burned for three days with a green flame and was not consumed. Our Lady appeared to a blind peasant beside a fountain one night, and when the priests fed him wine he described the vision in scriptural language.

The faithful seemed to detect a kind of malicious joy fermenting throughout the winter in the dwellings of the accursed Jews.

Strange things happened. Bands of dark wanderers, huge and black as bears, appeared simultaneously in several places. Even educated folk could sense at times a murmur gnawing inside them. There was no peace to be had.

In Clermont, in the year of the Incarnation of Our Lord Jesus Christ 1095, Pope Urban II summoned the flocks of God to an expedition to liberate the Holy Land from the hands of the infidel, and to expiate their sins through the hardships of the journey—for spiritual joy is achieved through suffering.

Early in the autumn of the following year, four days after the end of the vintage, the noble Count Guillaume of Touron set out at the head of a small troop of peasants, serfs, and outlaws from his estate near Avignon and headed toward the Holy Land, to take part in its deliverance and so to find peace of mind.

Besides the blight which had afflicted the vines and the shriveling of the grapes, and besides gigantic debts, there were other, more immediate reasons which moved the noble Count to set out on his journey. We are informed of these in the chronicle of an extraordinary young man who himself took part in the expedition, Claude, nicknamed 'Crookback.' He was a distant relative of the Count and had grown up on his estate.

This Claude was perhaps the adoptive heir of the childless Count, perhaps a mere hanger-on. He was literate and almost cultivated, though prone to violently alternating fits of depression and enthusiasm. He would give himself over by turns, restlessly and without any real satisfaction, to ascetic practices and to the delights of the flesh. He was a great believer in the power of the supernatural: he kept company with half-wits, fancying he found in them a holy spark, and much-thumbed books and peasant women alike fired him with a wild desire. His excesses of religious fervor and gloomy melancholy inspired feelings of contempt and loathing in others and consumed the very flesh from off his bones, kindling an evil flame in his eye.

As for the Count, he treated Claude Crookback with sullen toleration and ill-suppressed rudeness. Some uncertainty, in fact, prevailed at court about the status and privileges of this young but silver-haired fellow who had, apart from everything else, a violent and ridiculous love of cats and who was a passionate collector of women's jewelry.

Claude mentions in his chronicle, among the factors which prompted the Count to set out on his journey, certain events which occurred in swift succession in the course of the preceding year. 'At the beginning of the spring,' he writes, 'in the year of Our Lord's Incarnation 1096, the sin of arrogance raised its head among the peasantry. There occurred on our estate several cases of insolence and insubordination, such as the destruction of part of the meager crop, motivated by anger at its very meagerness; daggers were stolen, the river flooded, barns were fired, falling stars were seen, sorcery was practiced, and mischievous pranks were played. All this within the confines of our domain, apart from numerous crimes in the neighboring districts and even across the river. Indeed, it was found necessary to oil the torture wheel once again, and to put to the test several rebellious serfs, so as to quell the rising fever of violence, for suffering begets love. On our estate seven peasants and four witches were put to death. In the course of their torture their crimes came to light, and light purges all sin.

'In addition, during the spring our young mistress Louise of Beaumont showed the first signs of falling sickness, the very disease which had carried off her predecessor two years earlier.

'On Easter Day the Count carried his drinking beyond all reasonable limits, and on this occasion he did not succeed in soaring above the state of tipsy rage to the heights of drunken joy. There occurred episodes,' continues the chronicler in a rather veiled tone, 'such as what happened that night, when the Count smashed six valuable drinking vessels, family heirlooms; he hurled these gorgeous objects at the servingmen in reprisal for some fault whose nature was not clear. Injuries were done; blood was spilt. The Count made reparation for his error with constant silent prayers and fasting, but the fragments of the shattered goblets could not be pieced together—I have them all in my keeping still. What is done is done, and there is no going back.'

Claude also writes as follows:

'In the early days of the summer, in the course of the barley harvest, the Jewish agent fell under suspicion. He was put to death in consequence of his fervent protestations of innocence. The spectacle of the burning of the Jew might have served to dispel somewhat the anxiety and depression which had caught hold of us since the spring, but it so happened that the Jew, as he was being burnt, succeeded in upsetting everything by pronouncing a violent Jewish curse on Count Guillaume from the pyre. This terrible event occurred in the presence of the whole household, from the ailing lady down to the most ignorant servant girls. Obviously it was impossible to punish the wretch for his curses: it is in the nature of these Jews to burn only once.

'In the course of the summer our lady's condition grew worse and she began fading toward death. Without grace even love is of no avail. It was a pitiful spectacle. So grievous were her agonies, so loud her screams in the night, that the Count was finally compelled to shut up in the tower the most delicate of the flowers of his garden. Therefor was the Son of God meek and mild when He bore our sufferings upon Himself, that we might know and remember that the finest harvest of all is this, when the harsh scythe bites into the tenderest crop in God's world, and this was a sign for us. By night, by day, and by night the Count gave orders for vigils of prayer by the cell of our ailing lady.

'Our lady was young in years and her pale face seemed ever filled with wonder. Her limbs were delicate and she seemed completely transparent, as if made of spirit, not of base matter. She floated away downstream from us before our very eyes. Sometimes we could hear her voice raised in song; sometimes we secretly gathered up her tear-soaked handkerchief, and in the small hours of the morning we heard her cry out to the Blessed Virgin. Then her silence would rend the air. These days saw a severe deterioration in the affairs of the estate. The creditors were arming themselves, and even the peasantry nursed a muttering rebelliousness.

'All speech was hushed in our halls. So frail and white-faced did our lady appear that, kneeling at the foot of the cross, she seemed to us like Our Lady Herself. She was flickering and dying away. Meanwhile the Count withdrew into silence, and merely kept on buying more and more fine horses—far in excess of the needs of the fields and vineyards. He paid for them with parcels of woodland and orchards, since the money we had borrowed was being steadily eaten up.

'Early one morning our lady suddenly heard the gentle sound of the bells of the village church. She put her golden head out through the lattice, and when the sun rose she was found gathered into the bosom of the Saviour. I still keep her sandals in the chest in my room, together with two tiny bracelets and a green cross of pearls which she wore round her neck, a gorgeous object.'

The chronicle of this relation of the Count also contains some turbid musings, fraught with confusion, written in troubled and disconnected Latin. Some of them may be quoted here:

'We are touched by inanimate objects. There is a secret sign language which weaves a net between things. Not a leaf falls to the ground unless it is touched by some purpose. A man of the brooding type, such as my noble lord Guillaume de Touron, if he is but cut off for a while from the sphere of action, is immediately liable to come under the influence of the supernatural. If he is not found worthy of grace, it enters into his vitals like a gnawing poison, unseen, unfelt, but lethal. The anguish of vast plains scorched by the noonday sun, without a man to cast a shadow. Scents borne on the breeze. Woods, restful yet menacing. Perhaps the allure of the ocean. Or the tender, bitter silence of distant mountains. So a man of the finer breed, in the middle of his life, toward evening, as the wind drops, may suddenly pause and shrink back, shrink back listening with all his might, and as he listens he gnaws incessantly at his own soul.

'For all these reasons, then, and for others which cannot be put into words, Guillaume de Touron set out for the Holy Land, bent on taking part in its deliverance and thereby also on finding peace of mind.'

Chapter two

Slumped in his saddle like a weary huntsman, his features hewn of granite, his skull big and broad, the Count led his company up through the Rhone lands toward the town of St. Étienne. There, at St. Étienne, he meant to break the journey and pass a day or two. Claude Crookback supposes that he wanted to spend some time at the cathedral in solitary prayer, to ask the bishop's blessing on the expedition, and to buy fodder and arms. Perhaps he also intended to take on a few knights as mercenaries. The roads are fraught with dangers outside the city walls; the sword must hew out a passage for the forces of grace.

The Count rode on his mare, Mistral. His pace was still leisurely. This was not due to hesitancy, nor to that calm which follows the moment of self-dedication; it was simply a slow horizontal growth along the road. The mare Mistral was a massive, broad-built creature, just like her master. At first sight she seemed like a work horse: she could never be roused to the point of anger, thanks to a kind of feigned modesty which extended over all her movements, like a sort of inner deliberation—placid, ruminative, almost sanctimonious. But at a second, more penetrating glance—when one noticed, for instance, her capricious manner when being saddled or unsaddled—one could see quite clearly that just as it was impossible to arouse her, so it was completely and utterly impossible to enforce total submission on this mare Mistral.

And everywhere could he felt the creeping, fawning intensification of the forces of autumn on the plains and in the hills. The odors of the vintage everywhere accompanied the expedition on its way. It was like a constant melody, soft yet at the same time penetrating and persistent.

The signs of the drought and the blight on the vines were everywhere plain to see. The faces of the peasants bore expressions of muted, ill-suppressed malice.

Even in times of plenty these districts ever gaze up to the gray sky with a tight-lipped look: mud-spattered peasants, rotting roofs of thatch, clumsy crosses like the very faith of the region, blunt and strong, row upon row of black haystacks, and at dawn and at dusk there comes rolling from afar the sound of rustic bells, calling to the Saviour out of the depths.

At these twilight hours one could also make out the taut lines of powerful birds in flight. And their sudden screeching. In everything there could be seen the mounting evidence of a heavy, thick reality—or, at a second glance, the slight impulse of some abstract purpose.

Everything, even the silent, baffled docility of the plump peasant girls who paused to gaze from a safe distance at the company of men on horseback, everything was somehow open to several interpretations.

Had Guillaume de Touron considered the possible interpretations? If so, he did not show it on the surface. His few, brief words of command bore witness to an inner distance. It was as if he were sunk deep in a problem of logic or preoccupied with the checking of books which would not balance. Our chronicler, Claude, who frequently noticed his lord's silences, was sometimes inclined to attribute to him abstract speculations or spiritual exercises. In short, it was sometimes felt that the Count omitted to answer questions, or answered without being asked. 'Come here,' he would say. 'Put it there. Now. Fetch it. Forward.'

Those who heard these orders might easily have imagined that they were uttered by someone who was about to fall asleep, or who was struggling to rouse himself from a deep slumber.

Nevertheless, the man surrounded himself with a cool ring of lordliness, which needed neither effort nor stress: a strong, inborn quality, compelling fear and silence even while he slept, a crouching wolf.

An inborn quality. In Claude's chronicle one can read a short description of the appearance and bearing of the Count at the start of the expedition, and also a comparison which—after the manner of the chronicler —is rather fulsome:

'Truth to tell, the comportment of Count Guillaume de Touron was not only extremely natural and composed, but entirely free of doubts and excitements. It was like a gentle stream wending its way calmly among the meadows of a plain. Placid and leisurely it flows, never tearing at its banks or throwing up waves or spray, but everything which falls into its current is swept constantly on by a force which is neither friendly nor yet timid: a peaceful, inexorable stream.'

Chapter three

At dusk on the third day of their journey the band of believers reached the gates of St. Étienne. They handed over their weapons to the officer of the gate, they paid all the dues, both sacred and secular, they submitted to a personal inspection at the hands of the guards, lest there should be found among them an invalid or a Jew, and finally the Count and his men were permitted to enter the city. The ignorant folk stroked and chewed their beards at the sight of such plenty of women, priests, traders, and merchandise.

In the square behind the Hospice of the Sacred Heart, Guillaume de Touron reviewed his men. He gave orders for the horses to be well fed, set guards over the baggage and animals, distributed two pieces of silver per head and gave the men leave to disperse around the town until daybreak the next day, 'so that they might satisfy their needs with women and drink, and also purify their souls with prayer.'

The Count himself, after a slight hesitation, chose in the first place to make his way to the cathedral. Above all he sought peace of mind. As often happens to men who are looking for something the nature of which is unknown to them, he felt a kind of vague physical unrest, as if his body were rebelling against his soul and defiling it with evil vapors. His body was tough, massive, and compact, his head held slightly forward, as if the weight of the world hung more heavily upon him than upon the mass of ordinary believers.

On his way to the cathedral there passed through his mind the forms of the death of his two wives, the second and also the first. He contemplated the forms which death had taken like a man looking at the shapes of icicles in the winter. He felt no sorrow for these women, the second or the first, because neither had presented him with a son and heir. But he saw quite vividly that their death was the beginning of his own. He visualized his death as a far-off place to which one must go, climbing perhaps or breaking through by force, and he joined together with a blind and stubborn bond the words 'to redeem,' 'to be redeemed,' 'to set fire,' 'to go up in flames.' Summer by summer, almost day by day, he felt his blood running colder. He did not know the reason, but he silently yearned for simple elements—light, warmth, sand, fire, wind.

Meanwhile Claude Crookback went down to a house of ill repute on the edge of the town. He found a woman of easy virtue, dressed her up in his clothes and put his cloak around her, and handed her his dagger. Then he stretched out on the ground for her to trample on him, and begged to be tortured. While writhing with her, drenched with sweat, Claude screamed and laughed, cried and talked continuously. In the confused account which he composed that same night in his cell in the Hospice of the Sacred Heart he does not wallow in the details of his sin but limits himself to an enthusiastic description of the eternal power of grace. Does not the sun deign to be reflected even in pools of mire without withdrawing his reflection?

The worthy bishop of St. Étienne, a small, rotund, simple man, was sitting motionless in his study, contemplating his hands stretched out before him on the table, or perhaps contemplating the table itself, and cautiously digesting his food. Guillaume de Touron's expression as he suddenly entered the study, half-blocking the doorway with his bulk, was—as the bishop himself later described it in his diary—'clouded in a manner which implied either abstraction or concentration, two states of mind which are far harder to distinguish by their outward indications than is commonly supposed.'

After the Mass the bishop and his guest sat down to a meal. They permitted each other a small drink, after which they closeted themselves together in the library. The light of ten great candles in copper candlesticks wove intricate patterns on their faces, on the curved outlines of the objects in the room. It exaggerated every movement and translated it into a language of gloomy shadows. Here the bishop and his guest conducted a brief conversation which touched on the subjects of the quality of humility, the City of God, horses and hounds, the hardships of the journey and its chances of success, the Jews, the price of woodland, and the varieties of signs and wonders.

The knight soon fell silent and let the bishop of St. Étienne talk on alone. The bishop, as we read in the studied Latin of his diary, 'was delighted by the intelligent and thoroughly polite, yet extraordinarily restrained attentiveness' of his guest.

Finally, well after midnight, by the failing light of the candles, Count Guillaume de Touron requested and received absolution from the bishop of St. Étienne. The bishop also bestowed on his guest some useful information on the state of the roads, the subtlety of the Devil and the strategems by which it can be circumvented, the sources of the sacred river Jordan and the Sea of Galilee, the gold of the Jews, the abominable acts of the Greeks and the means of preserving oneself from them. It was an hour of shadowy silence. Out of the depths of the silence came a slight rustling, as if there were someone else in the cathedral, nursing a different intention.

The guest entrusted to the servant of God a donation for the use of the Church. Then he took his leave. He walked out into the warm darkness, into the realm of the night.

Before retiring chastely to his bed, the bishop made a point of adding a few lines to his diary, which took the form of a somewhat remarkable observation, even allowing for the lateness of the hour.

'I am prepared to swear on oath now,' writes the pious cleric, 'that the man did not utter more than a hundred words in the course of the four hours which he spent with me in this holy place. It is amazing, almost uncanny, that we did not remark this extreme silence until after the man had taken his leave and departed. His silence succeeded in disguising itself completely. This is the first time since we entered on our vocation,' the bishop wrote in astonishment, 'that we have granted absolution to a Christian man and even blessed his journey without his having felt himself obliged to confess to us even one slight sin of the many sins of which this world is so regrettably full. Worse still, the very strange and suspicious secretiveness with which Count Guillaume de Touron treated us remained concealed from us until after the man had left our presence. Naturally we could not chase after him and bring him back out of the darkness. We are obliged, then, even *post eventum*, to exercise to the full the faculty of strict justice, and to conclude here that it is likely that we have for once been deceived in a sly, calculating, distinctly un-Christian way.

'On the other hand, we are equally obliged to exercise the quality of mercy, and to record herein that his silence, in common with certain other signs of suffering which we fancied we observed on the countenance of Guillaume de Touron, may be interpreted as indications of humility and of spiritual suffering. And are not these two, humility and suffering,' thus the bishop of St.-Etienne piously concluded this entry in his journal, 'outstanding Christian virtues? May God have mercy upon us.'

Chapter four

The expedition set out from St. Étienne and turned eastward, toward Grenoble. They crossed the river and streamed through dense autumnal forests. For the autumn was cautiously gathering strength, as though first testing the powers of resistance of the river, of the hills and of the forest, before falling on them.

At the outskirts of the villages stood rugged, bowed peasants, gazing motionless from afar at the passing procession. The Jews, as though forewarned, abandoned their hovels and disappeared into the undergrowth before the approach of the expedition. Out of the darkness of the woods they seemed to be rousing the forces of evil against us by muttering spells and incantations.

How unaware we are, mere creatures of flesh and blood and humors, of the unseen, powerful web of God's actions around us!

Guillaume de Touron knew this, and so he told Claude in camp one night: Sometimes the curse of God comes like the caress of a woman's hand, and sometimes His blessing comes like a knife in the flesh. The appearance of a thing or its effect is not its essence.

Take the curse and the wrath which God unleashed against

the Jews. See how God's curse has refined this tribe. These people are fine and subtle; even our own language when it comes from their mouths is somehow suddenly turned to wine.

The thought of the Jews excited an inner panting in Count Guillaume de Touron—a strong, dark purpose, gloomy and filled with cold joy.

Claude Crookback, for his part, was idly musing about the wives of these Jews—warm, moist, brown velvet bitches.

The Jews, thought Guillaume de Touron, are stealthily nibbling away at us, like water eating away iron. This is the soothing touch, which melts unseen. Even the sword—our sword—passes through them as through a mass of turbid water which will slowly consume it.

Gracious Lord, have pity on Thy flock, for the forces of defilement rage enflamed all around us, and temptation encircles us, trying to break in. And the faith in our hearts is upright and cold, barren and very sad. Is it possible perhaps that a Jew has insinuated himself into our ranks by stealth?

Guillaume de Touron was suddenly overpowered by this suspicion, and he found himself waking out of his slumber. A warm thaw started to stir inside him, and wrought a change for the better. Perhaps he had been granted a sign or a hint. In his heart he seemed to say: 'here,' 'there,' 'now.'

The appearance of the expedition was distorted when reflected upside-down in the streams, or when seen from afar. Water and distance had the quality of turning any movement to utter mockery.

Along the lines of hills whose green grew ever darker appeared first of all three knights on horseback, wrapped in white cloaks. A rough black cross was embroidered on their cloaks in front and behind, as if they had been run through with swords and the wounds had long since turned black. They rode on tall, brown horses. From a distance it seemed as if the hooves of the horses hardly touched the ground.

Behind them rode the Count, surrounded by his retinue, mounted and clad in helmets and coats of mail. The Count himself was dressed in hunting gear and leaned on the saddle of his mare Mistral as though he found it exhausting to ride. Was he, as Claude says, already somewhat ill at this stage of the expedition? The question is a foolish one. Almost everyone knows that illness is a configuration of inner possibilities too numerous to count.

Claude, by contrast, was easily recognizable, both by his deformity and by his flashy yellow shield, glinting like false gold.

Behind the Count's retinue hurried some three dozen men on foot. In the rear guard trudged mules laden with provisions, wagons rolling on wooden wheels, slaves and camp followers, a few women who had attached themselves to the expedition, two cows plundered from farmers along the way, some goats, and at the tail end of the procession and on both its flanks dozens of dogs, skinny, misshapen, malicious mongrels, aimlessly darting hither and thither.

The motley cavalcade flowed past mournful autumn fields as if irresistibly drawn by some invisible lodestone.

The autumn was folding everything into the embrace of a thick mist. The gathering dampness spread over everything. It seemed as though the autumn were being malevolently formed according to a careful plan: a damp, dark condensation in the woods; a gray vapor in the valleys; a tense calm projecting quivering forms on the horizon. And still the rains held back.

The days, the nights, the hours of twilight in between, were like a dream journey in which distance becomes a malleable substance, always prone to be distorted. Even the wild shouts of joy of the rough good-for-nothings around the campfire at night were immediately absorbed into the distance and reflected back to us purged by the alchemy of autumn and melancholy, far slower and deeper sounds than when they left the mouths of those base fellows.

Sometimes, toward dawn, before the camp was woken out of its slumber by the clatter of iron pots, by the jangling of spurs and the neighing of horses, Claude would be flooded with piety and would rouse his lord for matins. Then, at the hour of prayer, the universe would reveal itself and would overpower everything with its unbelievable peace. This was a gloomy peace, the sadness of barren hills which are no longer hills but the very soul of hills, the earth arching up in longing to the clouds in a seductive gesture which no satisfaction will ever eradicate.

And in the depths of the silence, the body itself began suddenly to yearn for its own extinction. Fine vapor, it was felt, was the proper consistency. And the prayer struck home to the man at prayer.

Chapter five

A few times it happened that darkness fell while they were still in the depths of the forest. Then they would light a great fire in the middle and surround the camp with a close circle of small bonfires for fear of vampires, wolves, and demons.

If one looked upward one could see how the light of the fire was broken by the thick ceiling of leaves. Round about, wolves howled, foxes' eyes glinted, an evil bird screeched and shrieked. Or was it the wind. Or sinister imitations of the sound of fox, bird, and wind. Even the rustling of fallen leaves hinted perpetually at the certainty of another, a hostile camp whispering round about us and hedging us in. The forces of grace were being besieged.

The first signs of an approaching conflict were concrete enough. Dogs would go mad now and again and have to be put down with an arrow or a spear-thrust. A horse suddenly broke its halter in the night and galloped off into the wild darkness as if it had chosen to turn wolf. One of the whores who had attached themselves to the army burst into shrieks and did not stop screaming for two days and three nights, under the influence of some spell or incubus. In the end they were compelled to abandon her to the devil who had seized hold of her. One day the Christians came to a spring, and, being parched, they drank and let their horses and servants drink, not realizing that the water was polluted. It inflicted humiliating agonies on man and beast alike. Surely a Jew had mingled with the Christians in disguise, was walking along the way with us, and cursing us.

Even the villagers received us grimly. The travelers were compelled to extract provisions, women, and drink from the stubborn peasants by force of arms. Once or twice stiff skirmishes broke out in the villages and Christian blood was spilt in vain. The parsimony of these districts was coarse and sullen. Even for an expedition of knights traveling in the name of Jesus Christ to deliver the Holy Land the villagers would not open their fists without a stroke of the sword to extract charity by force from their clenched grasp.

And yet in several villages there were women who came of their own volition after dark and silently offered their bodies. These village women were huge and strong as horses. Their silence during the act, their stiff, stolid submission, was open to several interpretations—pride or modesty, dullness or rebellion. Claude, assailed by glimmerings of fevered fanaticism, would try his strength by admonishing these peasant women. He would rise and stand before them and speak with ecstatic piety of the Kingdom of Heaven, the corrupt nature of the flesh, of the happiness in store for those who give all with a cheerful spirit, for to him that giveth shall be given, and compassion shall be shown to him that hath compassion.

Who can tell the number of those scattered villages on the fringes of the forest, in valleys without so much as a name, in great gorges swathed in mist, in the winding courses of forgotten brooks and streams? 'It is God's will,' writes Claude in his chronicle of the journey, 'to scatter His flock to the ends of the earth so as to gather to His bosom once more on the Day of Judgment the few, the elect, the truly deserving.'

As for the Count, he drove his men just as he drove his mare Mistral. He did not give them his attention, yet his presence could not be forgotten for a moment. In his heart he was lonely. Remote from his fellow men. Remote from his surroundings, a stranger to the forest, ice cold. And now, in its remoteness, this soul would converse with itself on the necessity of love. To love, to be loved, to belong, to be—Guillaume de Touron felt a wild desire to overpower or crush some obstacle whose nature was hidden from him until the day when he would be permitted to be reborn anew. His shattered thoughts played with various images of death, of alienation, of breaking through. Like a drowning man struggling with his last reserves of strength to free himself from the grip of the water. But he did not know what the water was or how far it stretched.

Outwardly he merely seemed silent and watchful. Straining his senses to the utmost, in the hope of hearing a voice. Afraid to open his mouth and speak, lest he should miss the voice: he who speaks cannot listen. And yet Guillaume de Touron was endowed with a strange power over others. Despite his silence, he overran and choked everyone around him like a great creeper. Without intending to, he grasped and clung to everything, leaned on it with all his weight. It was a false impression that Count Guillaume de Touron, as often befalls men of his class, was a withdrawn and hesitant master, showing no reaction when his servants ran wild. A second glance would show that the reeds on which he leaned bent beneath him, while he, by the mere force of his nature, twisted and crushed them unawares.

From time to time he would conjure up an image of Jerusalem, drawing ever closer, but he would dismiss these inner visions, for they brought him no satisfaction.

In camp, at prayer, as they drank from the cask or from mountain streams, Guillaume de Touron would cast a gloomy eye over each man in turn, trying again and again to detect the hidden Jew.

By now his first suspicions had turned to utter certainty, as happens sometimes to a man who seems to hear in the distance a vague, menacing tune which causes him to wonder whether or not it is really there.

After a while, from the effort of listening, the tune begins to lead the listener astray, to come suddenly from inside him, from his very innards.

He surveyed his men, every single one of them, their expressions and gestures, eating, at play, in sleep, and on horseback. Is there any reason in looking for signs in the sensible sphere? And what is Jewish in a Jew—surely not any outward shape or form but some abstract quality. The contrast does not lie even in the affections of the soul. Simply this: a terrible, a malignant presence. Is not this the essence of treachery: to penetrate, to be within, to interfuse, to put out roots, and to flourish in what is most delicate. Like love, like carnal union. There is a Jew in our midst. Perhaps he had divided himself up, and insinuated himself partly here, partly there, so that not a man of us has escaped contagion.

Once, when the army had halted toward evening beside a Roman ruin whose remains were being eaten away by decay and strong roots, the Count turned to Claude Crookback with a question: Is it not written in one of those books that a wolf can insinuate himself so successfully into a flock of sheep that even a hunter cannot recognize him?

Claude's reply, perhaps in a slightly improved version, appears in his chronicle:

'I replied to this question from my lord the Count by means of a simple parable or allegory, in the spirit of the wisdom of the ancients. The sweetest apple is always the first to turn rotten. A wolf in sheep's clothing would naturally exaggerate his disguise. This is a sign for us: Who was it who embraced our Saviour and kissed His cheek and reveled in honeyed words and signs of love, if not he who had sold him for thirty pieces of silver, the traitor Judas Iscariot. The Devil is cunning, my lord, cunning and insidious, and we Christians are men of innocence. Without the grace of Heaven we are trapped, every one of us, in the snare set at our feet.'

Chapter six

A mong them there was a piper, Andrés Alvárez by name. He was devoted to the slaves and outcasts and harlots and believed in the power of his music to soften even the most unruly spirit. He even experimented with the horses and dogs. He had forsworn meat and wine, and wore a heavy stone on a chain round his neck to humble himself to the dust, for he thought of himself as 'meek and lowly.' Perhaps he was trying to purge his body of some sin he had committed or had intended to commit a long time before. He nicknamed himself 'Worthy of Death,' and wanted to be killed on the road to Jerusalem. Suspicion fell on this man. He was ordered to pass his hand through the fire so that it could be ascertained what he was. Because of his terror, and perhaps indeed out of joy at the purifying ordeal which lay ahead, he was seized with great excitement and was bathed in sweat. When he passed his hand through the fire, it was as wet as if it had been soaked in water, so that he was only slightly scorched, and the verdicts were divided. But seeing that this Andrés pleaded with the Count to have him put to death because he was tainted with impurity, they spared him and let him live so that he could be kept under further observation.

There were also three Celts, who were half brothers. They were the sons of one woman by three different fathers. These three displayed an unwholesome disposition to burst into horrifying laughter at things which were no laughing matter, such as a dead fox, the stump of an oak struck by lightning, or a sobbing woman. They were also in the habit of lighting a small fire of their own at night and huddling around it secretively, talking all the time in an unknown language, full of harsh consonants.

Every Sunday the three half brothers would celebrate an esoteric rite. Piling up heaps of stones, they would wring the neck of a bird and pour out its blood into a fire which they had lit in the hollow of the stones. Perhaps they used to conjure up by this means the soul of their mother.

The Celtic brothers were also gifted with extraordinary powers of marksmanship, which did more than anything else to attract to them the icy glances of the Count. Expertly they would amuse themselves by firing an arrow into the air and piercing it with another in mid-flight. Several times they hurled a stone in the dark and brought down a night bird in pitch darkness, guided by the sound of its wingbeats alone.

One evening Claude Crookback was sent to tell them to moderate their laughter, as befits men on a holy mission, to stop talking among themselves in their pagan tongue, and to allow him to inspect their baggage. In addition, Claude resolved inwardly to find a suitable opportunity to examine each of them while they were passing water so as to make certain that none of them was circumcised.

Claude himself, it must be admitted, loved these errands, because he felt himself humiliated by them. For the humble shall be exalted and the lowly of spirit shall be raised up.

From Grenoble the expedition continued to move slowly eastward.

The Count chose to keep away from the main roads. He was attracted to forgotten regions. Sometimes he even decided to abandon the lanes and to cut across the heathland and forest. It was not the shortest route that he preferred, but the most forsaken. In practice, Guillaume de Touron set his course afresh every morning: he simply rode in the direction of the sunrise, and continued riding until the rays of the setting sun struck his helmet from behind. He put a simple explanation on the laws of the universe: whoever moves toward the light moves toward the Holy City. Insofar as it was granted to this weary soul to feel love, he loved Jerusalem. He firmly believed that in Jerusalem it is possible to die and be born again pure.

And so, while the autumn beat on their backs with fists soft as a caress, the travelers crossed the foothills of the mountains, felt their way through misty glens, and gradually advanced down the slopes toward the valley of the river Po. There was not a man among them who had ever seen the sea. Perhaps they imagined that it would appear to them as an exceedingly broad river, that if they strained their eyes they would see the opposite shore and discern the suggested outline of towers, walls, lofty steeples, a high halo of light, a holy brightness hovering over the City of God on the other side.

Meanwhile, all along the way, they sustained themselves on what the villagers offered them at the sight of the sword. They made detours around the towns and the estates of noblemen, as if they were constantly avoiding an outstretched net.

Several times on the way they met other companies of knights also making their way to the Holy Land. The Count was not willing to join those who were greater than himself and would not condescend to annex to his band those who were smaller. As they had set out from their own land, so he wanted them to arrive at the Holy City: few but pure.

One day they were almost compelled to hew their way by force of arms. Near a small village by the name of Argentera, beside the well on the way into the village, Guillaume de Touron was surprised to come across a heavy force of crusaders, at least three times as large as his own band. These were Teutonic knights with a large crowd of followers, and at their head was a young knight, fair of face and haughty of mien, Albrecht of Brunswick by name.

This was a magnificent expedition: respectable matrons borne in litters curtained with silk, a company of elderly lords in costumes of scarlet, gold-buttoned, a company of young lords wearing long, pointed helmets tipped with a silver cross, attendants decked out in velvet liveries, banners and standards carried by scar-faced standard-bearers. There were also crowds of priests, jesters and easy women, beasts and animals. All this great abundance was carried in broad wagons the likes of which have not been seen in our country. The sides of the wagons were painted all round with detailed scenes from the lives of our Lord and His Apostles, all of whom the artist had chosen to portray with stern expressions.

Albrecht of Brunswick deigned to dismount first and present himself to the lesser lord. He delivered himself of a long succession of greetings in florid Latin. He also uttered words of enticement. It was clear that he proposed to take this smaller party which had crossed his path under his wing. But when, after the formulas of greeting were finished, Guillaume de Touron maintained a frigid reserve and refrained from fulfilling the obligations of Christian fellowship, even responding to his greetings as though they were also farewells, the German smiled a faint smile and gave orders to unseat the stranger from his horse and to annex his band by force.

Before he had finished issuing the order there was a clatter as every sword was drawn. Horses began to rear and neigh, and their skins rippled like pools of water in a breeze. A great movement took hold of the men, and glittered on spears and helmets. Instantly the band raised their instruments and started to play with fierce joy. Wild yet spectacular was the sudden melee of horses, banners, and accouterments, dust, shouts, and war cries, as if a colorful dance had suddenly broken loose on those gloomy plains. Even the cries of the first casualties of battle resembled from a distance the clamor of reveling merrymakers. Everyone, even the dying men, faithfully maintained a certain style from which they would not depart by a hair's breadth.

And so, quite soon, the knight from Brunswick said, 'Stay,' and the herald called, 'Stay.'

At once Guillaume de Touron, too, raised his visor. The music

28

stopped and the fighting died down. The men stood where they were, breathing heavily, trying to calm their quaking mounts. Soon they began to drink, and to offer one another German ale and Avignon wine from hairy flasks. The musicians, of their own accord, immediately began to play a different tune. While the officers were still busy separating the last hot-blooded skirmishers, laughter had spread all around. The warriors blasphemed and laughed.

Among the Germans there was a holy physician. He and his assistants went through the battlefield and picked out the wounded from the dead. He tended the wounded on both sides and the dead were cast all together into the well, after sufficient water had been drawn for everyone's needs. The casualties totaled fewer than a dozen dead, all from the lower elements on both sides, and their death did not mar the feelings of brotherhood which quickly sprang up of their own accord around common campfires. Those who forgive shall be themselves forgiven. As evening fell the priests celebrated a great Mass, and in the night both sides together slaughtered cattle, said grace, and ate and drank. Toward dawn they exchanged maidservants.

And so, toward dawn, Claude Crookback, drunk and foam-flecked, was sent to appease the knight from Brunswick with fifty pieces of silver as a toll and the price of peace, since Guillaume de Touron and his men were the smaller party.

Later, as the sun rose, Christian knight saluted Christian knight and both groups went their separate ways, holding high their banners and waving adieu. If sins had been committed, surely blood, prayer, and silver had made atonement. And the rain which came late in the morning, a very light and gentle rain, wiped everything away with its transparent fingers.

Chapter seven

Next day they came upon a Jewish peddler by the wayside. He had a pair of goats with him, and on his back was a knapsack. As the horsemen came downhill toward him he made no attempt to hide. He doffed his cap, smiled with all his might, and bowed three times, each time lower than the last. The procession drew to a halt. The Jew, too, stopped, and laid his sack on the ground. The Christians were silent. The wayfarer, too, kept silent and did not dare to utter a word. So he stood, by the side of the road, prepared to buy or to sell, to be slain or to deliver a polite reply to any remark which might be addressed to him. And he smiled with extreme concentration.

Claude Crookback said:

'Jew.'

The Jew said:

'Greetings, travelers. May your journey be blessed with success.' And immediately he tried again in another dialect and in another language, for he did not know which was their tongue.

Claude Crookback said:

'Jew, where are you going?'

And without waiting for a reply he added in a honeyed whisper:

'The sack. Open that sack.'

Before he had stopped speaking the three Celtic half brothers suddenly burst into shrill, loud laughter, very wild but entirely free of malice, as if they were being tickled under the armpits. The peddler opened his sack, bent down, and drew out an armful of knickknacks and gewgaws of the kind which are made to amuse small children, and said very happily:

'Everything cheap. Everything for coppers. Or we can arrange an exchange, for things no one wants any more.'

Claude asked:

'Why are you traveling, Jew? What makes you go from place to place?'

The Jew said:

'Are we alone in the world, gracious knight? Can a man choose for himself to go or not to go?'

Thereupon there was a silence. Even the Celtic brothers fell quiet. As if of her own accord, the mare Mistral moved forward and carried the Count into the center of the ring of horsemen. The smell of the horses' sweat spread around, pungent and menacing. The silence became more and more intense. A secret terror suddenly seized hold of the two goats, which were held by the Jew on a rope in his hand. Perhaps the stench of the horses brought them a premonition of evil, and the goats were alarmed. A twin bleating broke out, piercing and shrill as the ripping of cloth, as if a baby were being scorched by flames.

At this, all restraint was shattered. The Jew kicked one of the goats sharply, and Claude kicked the Jew. The peddler suddenly began giggling with all his might, his mouth gaping open from cheek to cheek. Then, radiating a politeness which was not of this world, he wiped his eyes dry with his sleeve and entreated the knights to accept everything, the goats and the merchandise, as a free gift in perpetuity, because men of every faith are ordered to love their fellow men, and there is one God over all of us. So he spoke, and his smile beneath his beard showed red as a wound. Count Guillaume de Touron made a sign with his finger that the gift should be accepted. The goats were taken, the sack was taken, and silence fell once more. Claude slowly raised his eyes toward the Count. The Count was gazing at the treetops, or through them to the patches of sky beyond. A whisper passed through the trees, thought better of it, and instantly fell quiet. Suddenly the Jew thrust his hand into the folds of his clothing and brought out a small packet.

'Take the money, too,' said the Jew, and held the packet out toward the Count. The knight took the packet with a weary gesture, closed his hand round it, and concentrated his gaze as if trying hard to discover what hint the shabby cloth held for him. There was a remote sadness at that moment in Guillaume de Touron's gaze. It was as if he were searching for something in the depths of his soul while being gradually shrouded in darkness. Perhaps he was filled with sorrow for himself. Finally he spoke, and he said with suppressed pain verging on warmth:

'Claude.'

Claude said:

'This is a Jew.'

The peddler said:

'I have given you everything and now I shall go happily on my way and bless you.'

Claude said:

'Now you shall not go and you shall not bless us.'

The peddler said:

'You are going to kill me.'

He said this without fear and without surprise, but rather like a man who has been searching in vain for a complicated solution to a complicated problem and suddenly discovers a simple solution. And Claude Crookback replied softly:

'Thou sayest.'

Once again silence filled the air. In the silence birds sang. Infected with the autumn, the land stretched to the farthest distance, quiet and broad, quiet and cold. The Jew moved his head up and down a few times, concentrating, contemplating, looking as if he wanted to ask a question. And finally he asked:

'How?'

'Go,' said Guillaume de Touron.

A moment later, as if mistrusting his voice, he wearily repeated:

'Go.'

The Jewish peddler stood as if he had not heard. He began to speak, and thought better of it. He raised his arms wide, and let them drop. He turned. He walked slowly downhill as though he still carried the heavy sack on his back. He did not look round. Cautiously he quickened his pace. Then, as he neared a bend in the road, he began to run, slowly, cunningly, bent forward, dragging his feet like a sick man about to stumble and fall.

But when he reached the bend he gave a sudden bound and redoubled his pace, disappearing now with amazing speed, tracing with great care a zigzag course, and did not stop running in zigzags even after the arrow hit him and lodged in his back between his shoulders. Then he stopped, twisted his arm round behind him, drew the arrow out of his flesh, and stood rocking backward and forward, holding the arrow before his eyes with both hands, as if a careful inspection was demanded of him. He stood staring at it until a second arrow dislodged the first from his grasp and pierced his forehead. Even now he stood where he was, and the arrow in his head stuck out in front, so that he looked like a stubborn ram, lowering his head to butt, his feet set firmly in the dust. Then the Jew uttered a single cry, not long and not very loud, and, as though he had finally decided to give in, he collapsed and fell on his back. He lay there without a tremor or a shudder.

The procession began to move on. Andrés Alvárez, the piper, traced a large cross with his finger over the fields and the forest and the expanse of sky. The women who followed the expedition stood for a moment beside the body, now growing cold, and one of them bent down and covered his face with the hem of his robe. Blood clung to the palms of her hands and the woman began to sob. Claude Crookback, who had moved for once to the rear of the procession, was overcome with a terrible compassion and walked behind the woman, comforting her in a soft voice with pious phrases, and so the two of them found some peace. In addition, that night they opened the peddler's sack and among a mass of old rags they discovered bracelets and earrings and women's sandals the likes of which had never been seen in the region of Avignon, extraordinarily beautiful, which could be fastened and unfastened by means of a perfectly charming and fascinating yet simple little catch.

Chapter eight

Autumn, a gray and patient monk, sent out silent, icy fingers and smoothed the face of the land. Cold winds began to blow down from the mountains to the north. They penetrated every covering, and the flesh stiffened at their touch. In several places toward dawn a fine, clear crust of ice had already begun to coat the surface of the water. The men's breath froze, caught in the hairs of their beards; their lips turned blue and cracked.

But the heavy rains of winter still held back, and the Count still hoped to reach the coast before all the roads became waterlogged. The sea held out the promise of a change, of some kind of a break. He looked forward to beholding in the sea the reflection of the Holy City, bristling with tall, insubstantial towers, glowing white as warm ice, ringed around with rocky crags and deserts, bathed in bright sunlight—and behind this light another light.

And yet sometimes the heart is smitten by a strange hesitation: Does Jerusalem really exist on the face of the earth, or is she perhaps nothing but a pure idea, which anyone who sets out to find in the substance will lose altogether?

They were passing through a monotonous gray landscape, like a long, low corridor. The melancholy of the frozen orchards around the villages was silent and terrible. To the outward eye all these plains stood open on every side as far as the horizon. And yet it was all blindly shuttered, and the travelers traveled on and on, and there was no way out.

Everything was overpowered by the fall. Sometimes the expedition marched for hours and hours on a moldering carpet of dead leaves. A venomous gloom took hold of men and beasts alike, a hidden, desperate gloom from which death itself would have come as a blessed relief. This soft, foul carpet, made up of rotting apple leaves and decomposing fodder, rustled crisply underfoot, producing a dull, monotonous melody which, after a few hours, imposed on knight and peasant alike a mood of silent madness.

So, like an inexorable nightmare, the silent procession advanced day after day over vast tracts of imaginary desert which at every gust of wind and every footstep sighed and murmured. The soul's lifeblood was on the point of shriveling and disintegrating.

No one now doubted the hidden presence of a Jew in the company. In camp at night servants and knights alike kept watch on one another, feigning sleep, starting at each footfall, craning to catch every sigh or whisper, crying out in their sleep, striving to decipher the cries of other sleepers. There were occasional brawls, and some took the precaution of sleeping with a knife clutched in their hand. Secret conspiracies were formed, allegations were made, and everyone girded himself with silence. A few vanished in the night and never reappeared. A servant slit the throat of another servant, was betrayed and beaten to death. Andrés Alvárez played on his pipe, but even his cheerful tunes tore at the heart and heightened the mood of despair.

All along the way there rose the stench of squalid villages. The cloying scent of a horse's rotting carcass or the putrid odor of a man's corpse decomposing in a field. Overhead stretched low, thick skies whose grayish hues strained toward a deeper shade of black.

In this envenomed world even the echo of distant bells was turned to keening. Such solitary birds as still remained stood motionless on the tips of wet branches, as if being gradually absorbed into the realm of the inanimate.

They crossed overgrown graveyards, trampling over gravestones coated with moss and lichen, sunk into the embrace of the heavy earth. At the head of these stones stood rough, crooked crosses, two sticks of wood held together by a wooden rivet. Those moldy crosses would crumble at a slight touch.

When the expedition halted at water holes to draw water, those who peered into the depths of the water might have caught sight of an element which was not water.

Far, far away on the steep mountain slopes one could see, for an instant, between patches of streaming mist, the vague outlines of stone-built fortifications—lingering monasteries, perhaps, or the remains of ancient castles ruined even before the coming of the Faith. Below them the river and its tributaries rushed furiously in their tangled courses, as if they, too, were desperately trying to escape.

Over everything there came at dusk a desolate, sinister power of incredible malignity, the screeching of birds of prey or wildcats. These regions were gradually being coated in rust, rotting with it to the point of death. And so Jerusalem ceased to be regarded as a destination, as the arena of glorious deeds. A change took place. Men would break the long silence to say 'In Jerusalem.'

And one man among them began to realize, with the gradual dawning of an inner illumination, that the Jerusalem they were seeking was not a city but the last hope of a guttering vitality.

Chapter nine

This chapter of Claude's chronicle bears unambiguous witness to the force of the destructive powers which continuously emanated from the hidden presence of a malicious element which had insinuated itself among the crusaders. No longer content with an external watch, they now appointed an internal watch as well. A few knights were detailed to eavesdrop unobtrusively. Others were instructed to keep watch on these. Claude Crookback was in a position to keep those whom he mistrusted away from the Count's presence and to surround him with those who met with his favor. Conspiracies, false accusations, and secret intrigues were rampant. In this thick, dank atmosphere of suspicion and malignant terror Claude blossomed and flourished like some swamp plant. And yet he, too, was infected by the thickening fear.

Claude wrote: 'There is a stranger in our midst. Every night as we all call on the name of Jesus Christ one of us calls with a false voice, and that man is Christ's enemy. One night in the third watch a hidden hand extinguished all the fires, and in the darkness there came a shout in a language which was not the language of Christian men. An enemy of Christ is concealed among us, a wolf among God's flock. That same hand which put out the fires in the night is also killing our horses, which are dying in agony one after another from an ailment which is completely unknown in our land. As we approach the villages the villagers are warned in advance to conceal their provisions, their women, and their horses in the forest. The Jews everywhere sense our approach, and the countryside, which is hostile to us, shelters them. There is an evil in our midst. Someone among us is not one of us. He has been sent to deliver us up to the forces of defilement. O God, have mercy upon us, grant us a sign before we all perish, body and soul. Is it not for Thy sake that we walk this path of hardship and suffering? Is it not to Thy City that we are journeying—and if we do not end there, where shall we end?

'The spirit of our men is already weakened by fear of the intrigue which is being fomented in our midst, and there are some on the fringes of our contingent who are planning to turn back the remaining horses and return home empty-handed. Our lord Guillaume de Touron now rides all alone some way ahead of the party and no longer looks round, as if it is all one to him whether the others are still following him or not, as if he is traveling on alone to Jerusalem.

'Three mornings ago the Count drew up all the travelers in a row, beginning with the knights and concluding with the servants, the hangers-on, and the women, and subjected everyone to a penetrating scrutiny. He ended by suddenly calling on the Jew to fall to his knees at that instant, in that very spot, whoever he might be. Then, in total silence, he turned his back on the men and mounted his mare, slowly, as if he were ill. At first light the next day one of the women was found with her throat cut and with the point of the cross which she wore round her neck buried in her breast. It was I myself who closed her eyes and drew the pointed cross out of her flesh, without wiping the blood off it. O God, whither art Thou leading Thy flock, and what will become of us tomorrow and the day after?'

And again Claude writes in his chronicle, in a spirit of humility and submission to divine judgment:

42

'In the course of this morning my lord the Count summoned me to follow him to the other side of a hillock. When we were out of sight of eavesdroppers my lord said to me, 'Claude, you know. Why do you keep silent?' And I swore in the name of Christ, and in the name of my lord's late sister, who was my father's wife before he married my mother, I swore that I did not know, and that I was very much afraid. Then my lord the Count continued in a voice at whose memory my heart is rent with love and terror, 'Claude—are you really Claude?'

'I record here the words with which I have cried out to God all day: O God, behold us. We are being consumed by evil. Deliver us, O Lord; Thou hearest and Thou canst prevail. Sinners though we be, have compassion upon us. Is it not toward Thee that we are journeying day and night?'

Happy is the man who pours his heart out in his prayer: even if he cries out of the depths his prayer is answered.

A few days later, when the expedition had made a detour round the walls of Tortona and was pressing on eastward, the plague left the horses and even the weather grew slightly warmer. The farmers yielded large numbers of horses which sufficed for riding until better ones could be found. In one of the villages the three Celts succeeded in sniffing out great hoards of good provisions, cheeses and rye and fodder, all in one cellar, with hardly any bloodshed. Along the way we came upon two mule drivers carrying casks of wine, and we enjoyed the wine for several days. We also met a mendicant monk who sprinkled us with holy water and renewed the blessings of the Church.

And so it seemed as if our fortunes had taken a turn for the better. We did not stint our prayers and thanksgivings. Even the winter rains not only continued to hold off, but even receded into the distance; for four days a benevolent sun shone down upon us. The Count distributed silver coins. The sound of singing was heard again as we set out in the morning, and Andrés Alvárez, the piper, played us merry tunes on his pipe. And at the same time we began to draw nearer to communities of Jews.

Chapter ten

We began to draw nearer to communities of Jews, and our days grew brighter. Activity brought with it a new spirit: discipline improved, and industry and inventiveness reappeared among us. Some of the blazes we lit fired our hearts with joy, and the thrill of the hunt roused our slumbering senses.

We were not too ambitious. We left the Jews of the towns to stronger contingents. Count Guillaume de Touron merely passed through the remoter districts, clearing, as it were, the outer extremities of the ground—the Jews of a forgotten village or a wayside inn, or a mill hidden in a valley. Thus there fell into his hands small bands of Jews of the runaway or wandering variety. Even so, the expedition did not interrupt its eastward progress, and did not turn aside to track down fugitives or to scent out booty. They plowed a single, straight furrow, not too broad. They did not even pause to look back and see what had been accomplished and what remained to be done. The Count imposed a strict discipline on his men, and refrained from lusting after bloodshed. That is not to say that they avoided plunder, only that the Count forbade his men to take pleasure in it—and the suppressed pleasure whispered seductively.

Claude mentions in his narrative one Jewish woman, resembling a she-wolf, who, with her baby, was rooted out of her lair in the depths of a haystack. She snarled, and her fangs were whiter and sharper than human teeth. She hissed violently, as if she meant to bite or spit venom. Her breast heaved under her brown dress with a turbulence such as Claude had witnessed before only in the throes of physical ecstasy or in women who had seen a vision of a saint demanding that they throw themselves on the fire.

This Jewess even managed to keep at bay the ring of Christians who had closed round her. Not a man dared to approach within reach of claw or tooth. She stood alone in the center, and her face wore an expression which resembled a yawn. A second glance showed that this was no yawn.

She began to wheel round slowly, bent over, the baby clutched in the claws of one hand, the other hand held out in front, the fingers hooked like the talons of a bird of prey. Her movement suggested that of a scorpion or a crab. Even if Claude imagined that this Jewess was about to pounce and tear out their eyes with her nails, she did not do so. Instead, she suddenly hurled her screaming child into the arms of the youngest of the three Celts, and threw herself down, rolling in the dust as if she had already been slaughtered. She did all this in complete silence, without pleading or crying, but in a fierce convulsion. Claude Crookback struggled with all his might to suppress the sobs rising in his throat. A blind, feverish urge almost forced him to fall to the ground and roll in the dust like her and kiss the soles of her feet and be trampled on by the soles of her feet. This urge burned in his veins like a flaming fury, and yet it was not fury. Hot tears ran down his beard as he put this she-wolf out of her misery with a short, sharp blow, thus sparing her the agonies of a long-drawn-out death and relieving her of the ugly sight of the crushing of the child's head, a sight both sordid and distasteful to a sensitive soul.

The region was dotted with Jewish communities. There were some towns here which had opened their doors wide to them, in defiance of the ancient curse. These Jews had put down deep roots to drink the innermost sap, and were flourishing vigorously. They were endowed with prodigious powers of suckling and growing. In these villages numerous families of Jews had spread, buying and selling, hiring and letting. They had a total monopoly on the oil and flax. Slowly, calculating and relentless, they were expanding into wool and wax, putting out feelers toward perfumes and ales, timber and spices.

Outwardly they were calm, but a closer inspection would have betrayed a nervous muscular spasm in their faces, like the ripples on the skin of a deer standing in feigned repose, poised for flight. Our language flowed from the mouths of these Jews as smooth as oil. Our silver seemed to pass into their hands of its own accord, following the natural tendency of things to roll downhill.

Thus the Jews were past masters at gathering and hoarding, exchanging one thing for another at a favorable moment and concealing one thing inside another in times of apprehension. They seemed devilishly dexterous, evasive by the very nature of their breed. The very ground seemed to become pliant under their feet, and they exuded over everything around them a kind of sticky, transparent resin. They could arouse in the Christians sympathy or confidence, terror or amusement at their will. They were the pipers and we were the pipe in their hands, we were the dancing bear.

Many peasants in these regions put their faith in the Jews. Knights enticed followers to accompany them to Jerusalem with silver borrowed from the Jews. The wounds of our Lord and Saviour opened anew at the sight, and His blood was spilled afresh. Even great lords, even priests and bishops were accustomed in these parts to invite Jews into their very hearths, and unawares they slowly sold their souls. Some even trusted the Jews with power. So it happened that hereabouts certain Jews had risen to such heights as to be able to exercise power behind the scenes, and to pass on moral contagion to the Christians. Twice Guillaume de Touron's band was met on the way by armed guards or even tainted priests, their swords raised as a barrier between him and the Jews, setting at nought God's curse.

In short, these Jews had raised up a shadow-Judaea at the foot of the Cross, spreading all around, extending the reign of hostile forces into Christian lands. To borrow a simile which recurs several times in Claude Crookback's chronicle, the Jews were like a band of strange minstrels wandering noisily through a primeval forest. Undoubtedly there was some sweet and desolate enchantment in their music, but the forest had a music of its own, deep and dim, and it would not tolerate for long another tune.

One day Guillaume de Touron rode at the head of his men into a group of hovels, on the edge of a small village called Ariogolo, which were inhabited by Jews.

As often happened, they had scented what was coming and had escaped into the forest. A single spokesman came to meet the knights, to negotiate a ransom and to obtain sympathy. He also wanted to rescue from the fire a houseful of old books, some of which, he claimed, were a thousand years old. Jewish books, written backwards.

This man was lean and lanky; his beard was fair and his shoulders strong. Even in his manner there was nothing to suggest his base origin. His movements were few and economical, he seemed calm, and he spoke in the measured tones of one who loves words and is their master. He came out of the house toward the leading horsemen and inquired who was in command. Before they had time to speak or move, his glance rested on the Count and he said, 'He is the one.' Then he strode boldly between the horses, almost brushing them with his shoulders, took up his stand in front of our lord Guillaume de Touron, and said:

'I was looking for you, my lord. This is your expedition.'

The knight squinted, weighing with his glance the figure before him, and immediately perceived the strength of his determination. He twisted his lips and said:

'You were looking for me.'

'I was looking for you, my lord.'

'What are you offering, Jew, and what do you want to take?'

'A houseful of holy books. And if you are in great need of money, then all the rest of our houses. Payment in cash.'

A faint smile, grim and rare, passed over Guillaume de Touron's face and vanished. For an instant a peasantlike expression, full of greed and loathing, played round his lips. Then his glance froze. Coldly he said:

'Gold. Copper coin has no currency in the places to which I am going.'

The man said:

'Great quantities of gold.'

Guillaume de Touron said:

'You, Jew, stand on the house which you want to save from the fire, and the fire, by God's grace, will choose what to consume and what to leave untouched.'

The Jew said:

'Very well. You set fire to the southern side. The wind is blowing from the north. By God's grace there is a broad stream in between. The fire, as you say, will choose, by God's grace, what to consume and what to leave untouched.'

The Count paused. Once again a dry smile flitted across his face. Then, twice as stern, he said:

'My dear Jew, you are not afraid. Why are you not afraid of me?'

As if with a sudden sympathy the Jew uttered a short, bright laugh, carefully modulated by deep insight, and answered:

'I am giving, my lord, and you want to take.'

'And if I take and then kill and burn?'

'But you will swear, my lord, in the name of your Saviour. Before you swear you shall not see the gold.'

'And if I take by force, Jew?'

'You and I, my lord, are in the hands of a power which is greater than you or me.'

'Well then,' said Guillaume de Touron, in a dark tone of voice. 'Well then, give me the gold. Right away. You have spoken long enough. Give it to me now.'

As the Count uttered these words the nearest horsemen began to touch the Jew lightly with the tips of their lances, as if testing the thickness of the bark on a tree trunk.

The man said:

'The gold is buried in the field and the spot is buried in my heart.'

Guillaume de Touron said:

'Then get up and go to the place. Now.'

The Jew shook his head in resignation, as if disappointed at the clumsy narrow-mindedness displayed by his interlocutor. He said with exaggerated deliberateness, in the tone one would use with a stubborn peasant:

'But my lord, I have not yet had your lordship's oath. Your time is short and your way is long.'

'Go,' said the Count. 'Go and lead me to the house you spoke of.'

The handsome Jew motioned with his chin.

'That is the one. The books are there.'

The knight raised his voice slightly, and, calling to Claude Crookback, he said:

'Claude, have that house and all the houses burnt, and see that the Jew is not killed quickly, but slowly and patiently, and meanwhile tell them to turn the horses out into the field to graze and to send the servants down to the river to wash themselves before Mass—yesterday they stank to high heaven.'

They began to beat the Jew at noon. Toward evening they branded him with red-hot irons. Then they soused him in salt water and asked him about Judas and Pontius Pilate and Caiaphas. They took him out of the salt water and crushed his testicles, as Claude had read in one of the books when he was a boy, and as it was written in the same book they made him drink the salty water in which he had been immersed. Later, when they were dealing with his fingers, they questioned him on the subject of the types and allegories of Jesus Christ of which the Old Testament is full. As the twilight came on they put out both his eyes, and then, finally, he opened his mouth and asked them whether, if he showed them the place where the treasure was buried, they would promise to kill him instantly, and Claude Crookback gave his word.

In the dark the treasure was dug up, and it turned out that the Jew had not lied and the treasure was very rich indeed. Then the Count told Claude to carry out his promise. The hour, he said, was advanced, and it was not fitting to delay vespers any longer, because the fire, which had burned right through the village, was dying down and the smoke was interfering with their breathing and making their eyes smart. And so they thrust a lance through the tortured body from back to chest. But the Jew went on crawling blindly hither and thither, and his blood spurted out, and he continued murmuring. So they beat him over the head with an ax haft and called him dead. The Jew, however, was not dead. He sighed deeply through the hole in his lungs, and large pink bubbles came out of him and burst. Then they stabbed him again in the chest, but apparently they missed his heart. The broken relic of a man raised a leg in the air and kicked about furiously. The people who were crowded around him wiped the sweat from their brows and consulted with one another, then ordered the servants to throw the tortured body onto the smoldering fire.

But the ignorant serfs were already seized with superstitious panic, suspecting witchcraft or portents, and stubbornly refused to touch it with their hands. Finally Andrés Alvárez, the piper, drew near, he who carried always a heavy stone tied around his neck to mortify his flesh. Alvárez fetched a long pole and pushed and rolled the remains of the palpitating body into a shallow pool. The spokesman of the Jews lay bubbling in the water. Even after vespers he had not given up the ghost.

The Count gave orders to put off halting for the night and to ride on by the light of the moon, for the moon had come out, yellow and round and of enormous size. I gave my word, thought Claude, and I did not keep it, because the task did not lie within human power, and if it was the hand of the Almighty, then who am I? Not a leaf falls to the ground without being touched by a purpose, and it is not for us to know what that purpose is. So it was by God's purpose that our Saviour died on the Cross, for it was God's will that the traitor should betray Christ so that the Saviour should bear our sins and carry out afflictions.

For four days more Guillaume de Touron and his men

continued to plow the wild earth with their faith and to root out the hostile forces from the world. And at the end of four days, with fists of icy fury, the great rains of winter began to beat down.

Chapter eleven

The great rains of winter beat down violently and smote the earth. The vault of heaven itself seemed to collapse as the gray slivers of lead came down. The storm howled wildly in the forest, uprooting ancient trees, shattering roofs, and whipping the surface of the lakes into a frenzy.

So furious was the gale that it caught up wild ducks and hurled them against the mountainside. The water, usually a mild and submissive element, suddenly clenched into a fist and rose up against the massive rocks, toppling them with a single blow. All the rivers ran riot, seething and storming their banks.

Lightning flashed frenziedly from horizon to horizon, drawing dazzling, drunken designs over the whole width of the heavens. The thunder, in its turn, responded with its weird and menacing amen.

Now the wind would wrest the steeple from a village church and sport with it, carrying it off entire. The airborne bell flew swiftly past, ringing high and forlorn above hills, rivers, and forests until it was lost in the distance.

In the midst of the maelstrom at least one side of order or

design could be dimly discerned. All these tormenting forces worked with one accord toward rendering everything round, eliminating and exterminating anything which was pointed with all the violence of their flow, bending mercilessly everything upright or projecting, tearing at whatever was angular and forcing it to become curved.

The tempest eroded and rounded off the heaps of dust, the breakers on the lakes, the backs of men scurrying with their last strength to find shelter.

Those wild powers which had burst forth to subdue the whole land were totally hostile to cross, steeple, and lance, horse and man.

In the afternoon the wind veered round. The air was filled with large snowflakes. After the snow came the hail. By dusk the earth shone white. All night long the lightning played on the surface of the snow with a dazzling flame of blue—a terrible blue flame. Next morning the snow continued to fall, and piled up deeper still. Whatever the storm had left standing the snow rounded and curved. The whole land was silently subdued and transformed. Nothing could stand in the way of the hostile forces. A new power reigned over the earth.

In that pallid glare the whole battered company fell to its knees in the snow and prayed to the Savour. Lost as they were in that luminous wilderness, shrouded in banks of gray clouds swept about by the wind, perhaps there took shape in some of their minds a tentative vision of Jerusalem.

Chapter twelve

They went on walking till dusk, seeking shelter from those simple elements which buffeted the flesh and penetrated deeper to conquer the sensitive soul: the pouring rain, the knife-edged wind, the blinding light, the silence. Everything was stripped bare. A handful of wandering fugitives. A long flight. A trap.

In the afternoon the wanderers found a roof to shelter them. This was a broken-down, abandoned monastery, a stone fortress on the rocks of a remote mountain slope. Many years before, perhaps in times of plague, the last monks had fled to die elsewhere.

The building was constructed on an absurd, melancholy plan. A steeply inclined wall, enclosing no other building but simply closing in on itself, in whose thickness were dug myriad low cells and warrens of winding passages, spiral staircases, recesses, doorways, underground vaults lost in darkness. There was also a gloomy chapel, disproportionately long, like a narrow, curved corridor leading nowhere but to its own end. The very form of the place was consumed with contradiction.

Neglect had eaten away at everything, at the crude stone walls and the Latin inscriptions, broken by cracks and crevices, which spoke darkly of the resurrection of the dead and the delusion of earthly delights.

On the door of the monastery one could make out a notice written in the local dialect addressed to intending invaders, appealing to their religious feelings, cursing them violently and warning of the danger of plague. The writing was being eaten away by mold and rust.

Guillaume de Touron and his men broke down the door and went inside. The Count gave orders to unload, light a fire, and shelter here until the roads became passable. He was troubled or distracted as he issued his instructions, interspersing orders to ration provisions, take good care of the horses, and clean the tackle with vague reflections on the subject of walking on water, urgent messages to the Greeks, remarks about sleep as a simple escape from space and time, adding an obscure comment on the blight which had affected the vines and the rotting of the lower layers of earth beneath the topsoil.

The men did not speak, but the walls began to make their voices heard. While the Count was talking, the passages, doorways, and recesses sent back a hollow echo. They re-echoed and amplified a word here and there to a suspicious degree. When Guillaume de Touro finished speaking, the building intensified the silence.

The walls were all in the grip of a gradual decay. Weeds burrowed in the crevices of the stone, nibbling greedily at the rot, their bloated growth forcing up the flagstones, and as they burrowed they almost seemed to squelch noisily, as if the building were composed of marrowbones at which the plants were lustily sucking.

And the smells. A pungent stench of ancient incense lingering in the cracks in the stones came and went by turns.

The servants dispersed into the recesses and passageways, not searching, not finding, startled at meeting each other suddenly in the twists of the tunnels, trying the echo and being filled with terror at the result, lighting fires in the hollows. The smoke spread out along the ground, disturbing scurrying insects and night birds or monstrous bats. At the end of several days it was impossible to count the men or keep them in order. One or two were stricken with silent madness, wandering in the dark passages without a torch until their shouts died down and they were forgotten. All count was lost of the days.

Outside the loopholes, the realm of winter stretched to the far distance, endless tracts of snow on which the howling wind played a melody of darkness. The torrents of water had broken down all the bridges. Clearly there was no hope of escape until some change took place.

All day long the men played dice. When it grew dark they lit a fire, which they fed by tearing off the doors and hacking away the framework with their axes. After that they burned the furniture and fittings of the chapel. Finally, they even began to break down the roof beams to make a bigger fire so as to ward off the cold drafts which blew in through the roof, which they were progressively demolishing.

These roof beams were damp and musty. The fire drew out of them a simmering, hissing sizzle, as if men were being roasted alive each night.

Meanwhile, subjected to the influence of idleness and boredom, the servants progressively deteriorated. They began to degenerate at first from excess of ale, and when supplies of ale ran out they degenerated twice as fast from want of it. In the absence of farmers' wives it soon became evident that the women who accompanied the expedition were too few. They were squabbled over and squabbled with until some of them were killed and the rest fled into the snow. One of them killed three of her companions before they found her hiding in an alcove and slit her throat.

Even after the women had left the men did not mend their ways. The sooty walls were covered with obscene drawings. Here and there, when no one was watching, a man would desecrate one of the crosses, until they had to make do with the crosses of iron and feed the flames with the remains of the wooden ones.

Only the divine office was observed by everyone with an enthusiasm bordering on the fanatical. Morning and evening they would emerge from their various hiding places and gather together to pray ecstatically. On the days which they considered, according to their halting reckoning, to be Sundays, they passed half the day devoutly in prayer. The lower elements burst into noisy weeping as they prayed. Sometimes Guillaume de Touron would deliver a feverish, rambling address, exhorting his men to love him, to love one another, to love the horses which were perishing from the cold, to love their own flesh and their own blood, since their flesh was not their flesh, nor their blood their blood. Claude Crookback, for his part, was steadily amassing a power of his own. He encouraged some of the servants to come to him and confess their old sins, all of which occasioned in him lunatic delight. His chronicle bears witness to a morbid fascination with the nature of the body and its peculiarities.

Days and weeks went by. The last of the better elements in the party were disappearing into the snow to find their own way home. Those who remained battled with hordes of ravens which had also taken refuge there from the cold. They brought them down with arrows and stones, but others kept coming until the soul grew weary of them.

Outside, day after day, the soft, slushy snow piled up on the ground, and at night the wind beat relentlessly at the walls, dislodging loose stones and beams.

Worst of all, the Count was changing. Compassion took hold of him day by day. Something strange, a kind of hesitancy almost amounting to tenderness, suddenly came over him.

Chapter thirteen

He would wake from a long sleep (he dozed for long periods of the day and night), get up, and begin to perform acts of kindness. In the first place, he shook off all his old suspicions and seemed to take pride in the handful of men who accompanied him to Jerusalem. Secondly, he sought opportunities to exercise forgiveness. If he saw one of the men weakening, he would lay a hand on his shoulder and speak briefly and softly against sin. He began to address some of the more despicable characters as 'brother.' From time to time he would pay frenzied visits to his mare Mistral, give her water to drink from his own cupped palms, and groom her with his fingers. On one occasion he assembled everybody in the broken-down chapel, held a kind of Mass, and solemnly adopted Claude Crookback as his son. If Claude had not restrained him, he would have gone on to adopt several more of those present. To judge by his appearance, he was a sick man, but in terms of physical strength he was stronger than any man there, the three Celts included. It occurred to him to erect a sort of dais at one end of the chapel, and for several days he moved stones and fetched heavy planks. Then he suddenly stopped, and instead tried to induce the most ignorant men to learn Latin, and give up speaking 'those Jewish languages.' Once he fell to his knees, took off his shirt, and wrapped it round the foot of the eldest of the three Celts, a remarkable action, since the foot, though naturally unwashed, was in no way injured.

He demanded the constant companionship of Claude Crook-back. At first he implored Claude to regale him with extracts from the writings of the ancient sages. After a time, he would wake up in a panic and call for Claude, and eventually he was unable to fall asleep without resting his head in Claude's lap. Claude, as was his wont, would talk on and on, and since he met with no rebuke he talked even more than usual. Day by day authority passed from the Count to his adopted son, so that soon he could starve or flog men at his own discretion as the fancy took him. In his chronicle he wrote: 'Earth, men, snow, suffering, death, all of these are but an allegory of the Kingdom of Heaven, toward which I am making my way, in a straight line, turning aside neither to the right hand nor to the left, and with a joyful spirit.'

Then the snow stopped, and once more the winter rain fell day and night, in a tedious, unrelenting downpour. The snow began to melt on the hilltops. Thick mud covered the countryside. The cold became damper, a fetid, poisonous frost. Here and there traces of the road reappeared, winding among the hills. The road was waterlogged. Even in moments of despair, it was impossible to consider resuming the journey.

Within the ruined monastery supplies of food began to fail. Once or twice knives were drawn when the rotten rations were distributed. A foul disease broke out, which caused all of them unbearable sufferings and torments.

One night a pack of wolves stole in, wild with hunger. Silently the wolves swarmed through the dark and winding passages, broke into the cellars, and tore the last remaining horses limb from limb. If the scent of the wolves had not roused the three Celts from their slumber, we should all have been in danger of our lives. The Celts leapt to their feet and fell on the beasts of prey with lances, torches, shouts, knives, and stones. In the firelight even the men's expression seemed wolf like.

After this incident Claude Crookback instituted a night watch. The men would gather together at night to sleep surrounded by heaps of glowing embers. The guards prevented the wolves from creeping in again, but they were powerless to prevent the terror caused by the howling which was borne in on the night wind, piercing the very marrow of the soul. And the soul contracted and responded with an inner howling of its own.

Early one morning they caught sight in the distance of a dim form moving across the snow. It was a traveler, moving past slowly on the horizon, holding himself erect, feeling his way, a tall man wrapped in a black cloak, his head hidden by a black cowl. A wandering ascetic, perhaps, or a mendicant monk. The form did not respond to our cries and did not alter its course. The stranger passed before our gaze, pressing on slowly through the soft snow toward the opposite horizon. Maybe he was deaf, or bound by a vow of silence. Besides him no human form appeared all through the winter.

The cold grew more and more intense, stretching to the very limits of its strength. The men's bodies were covered with chilblains. Those horses which had been rescued from the fangs of the wolves perished in one day. Their flesh was eaten half-raw, because there was hardly any fuel left to feed the fire.

A spirit of rebelliousness gradually reared its head, restrained as yet but menacing. Servants, their eyes inflamed, whispered together in corners. If Claude Crookback walked past they would suddenly fall silent or hastily roll their dice. Whispers stalked about in the night darkness.

One day Andrés Alvárez risked his life climbing to the top of the crumbling belfry. He succeeded in setting the great bells to rights and fitting them with new ropes. He believed in the power of the bells to drive out the spirit of defilement and to put new heart into the men. But when Andrés slithered down from the belfry and pulled on the ropes the chimes which rang out were broken, ailing, blood-chilling. And from every corner of the tumble-down monastery arose waves of echoes, hoarse and pitiless.

And so they abandoned the bells and bade Andrés Alvárez, the piper, pipe away and still the murmurs of the silence.

Andrés's playing could stir the heartstrings. His melodies caressed his hearers like a hand. Something stirred and softened within them. The firelight flickered gloomily on the circle of shadowy faces, coarse-featured and shaggy. As the notes rang out, a kind of spasm or passing shudder played round those cracked lips. The tenderness was almost more than they could bear. Like stones frozen in a sheet of ice, which the slightest touch of warmth would shatter. Andrés Alvárez aroused in them a kind of craving, a repressed yearning. Suddenly someone in the circle of listeners would burst out screaming as if he had been stabbed. It was the scream of a wounded man who recovers consciousness and all of a sudden becomes aware of his pain.

His tunes were simple ones, such as one hears in the country in summertime, and from time to time Andrés would break into a soft, warm song, like the songs which peasant girls sing when they fancy that no one is listening. Some of the men joined in and sang with Andrés as if their lives had reopened with the song. Even Guillaume de Touron was stirred. This dwindling man sank his chin on his chest, and a last light passed through him. He remembered his wife, not the lady Louise of Beaumont, who had died that summer of falling sickness, but his first wife, Anna Maria. She was only a child when she was brought and presented to him, and he too was a mere lad. She was beautiful but silent as he first saw her standing in the gateway, he looking at her, she looking down at her slippers or at the ground. And he recalled now, in this twilight, how he had taken her hand and led her out onto the estate, to the orchards and vineyards and pastures, and then into the woods, as his forefathers before him had been accustomed to lead their brides on their arrival. He recalled her dress, the color of oleander, and the startled look in her eyes, and the ripples of panic racing over her skin as over that of a quiet young filly. He recalled her prolonged silence, and his own silence, and the singing of the birds, the treetops dyed by the rays of the sinking sun, the blossom in the orchards with its scent, for it was spring, and the tranquillity of the streams caressed by the scents of evening. Anna Maria walked behind him, and he let go of her hand, which was trembling. Then, in a frenzy, he suddenly determined to make her laugh. He started neighing like a horse and howling like a jackal, went down on all fours and imitated a deer in flight and a bear in pursuit, then suddenly threw himself from a high rock into the stream below, emerged dripping wet, and fell panting at her feet, giving a perfect imitation of a dog begging to be patted. How pure was that distant silence! Then, giving in, she laughed and touched his hand with her finger tips, and he, a wet, fawning dog, nuzzled her hand with his face. As his lips touched her fingers it happened, and Anna Maria said, 'You, you, you.'

Guillaume de Touron closed his eyes and gazed blindly at Andrés Alvárez, the piper. His heart told him that this place was strange and that even Jerusalem was not the goal of this journey but of another journey, no journey at all, no City of God, and perhaps Andrés was the hidden Jew, or perhaps not Andrés but he himself, for truth is so pure and only the eyes are blind, fire is not fire, snow is not snow, stones are thoughts and the wind is wine and wine is silence, prayers are fingers, pain is a bridge and death is home, is the touch, is the warm tinkling song 'You, you, you.'

Outside, as a counterpoint to the melody of Andrés, snow and despair once more fell softly, smothering everything with a kiss of unbelievable tenderness. So it was that Count Guillaume de Touron stopped the music and said:

'Claude, this piper is not one of us.'

Claude said:

'Father, have you not known Andrés from his youth? Did his grandfather not dandle you on his knee when you were a child?'

The Count said:

'Claude, why do you insist on shielding this Jew from me? He is hounding us, and it is his fault that we are lost.'

Andrés said: 'My lord.'

The Count, deep in thought, said sorrowfully, as if from a

distance: 'Andrés, you are dear to me, you are a dearly beloved Jew, Andrés, and I must kill you so that you die.'

Andrés Alvárez did not plead for his life, but curled up with his head between his knees and did not move. The Count rose, took up his spear, and stood beside Andrés. He leaned on the spear, his eyes closed. He was pondering or hesitating. He leaned harder on the spear, and a sigh escaped from his throat. He leaned harder still, the spear passed through his body and, as if clasped in an invisible embrace, he collapsed and lay still.

After the Count's death there were two more flights into the snow. Most of the servants vanished, taking with them what little food was left. Claude Crookback, leader of a party of nine crusaders, wrote, with a trembling hand, his eyes blazing out of a beard smeared with saliva: 'The miracle is delayed. Claude is humbled to the dust, the saintly Claude is plunged into the depths of the abyss, but beyond the mire there shines a light, and I am steadily making my way toward it, to be purged in it to the very limits of the flesh.'

The horror of those last nights. The faces of men whose teeth are rotted, whose lips are eaten away by cold. They shone white as skulls in the light of the night. The screaming. The laughter. They were turned to beasts, mauling their flesh with their teeth, falling to emaciated knees to worship the lightning which flashed across the night sky. And the visions. A luminous procession above their heads, figures of pallid ghosts, glimmering from the farthermost frozen distance.

On the last night there was a sign. Through the holes in the roof the dark clouds were seen to part slightly, revealing faint stars, and beyond the stars, a halo.

And so, finally, without horses, without clothes or provisions, without women and without wine, the cold tearing at their bare feet, to rise up and go to Jerusalem. Surely it was thus that they should have set out at the start.

Nine quivering silhouettes, Claude Crookback trudging in front, Andrés, the three brothers, four servants whose minds were long since unhinged, through meadows shining white from horizon to horizon, walking over the white earth under a white sky, on and on.

Not turning homeward—they had given up all thought of human habitation. Not even toward Jerusalem, which is not a place but disembodied love. Shedding their bodies, they made their way, growing ever purer, into the heart of the music of the bells and beyond to the choirs of angels and yet farther, leaving behind their loathsome flesh and streaming onward, a jet of whiteness on a white canvas, an abstract purpose, a fleeting vapor, perhaps peace.

Late Love

Chapter one

I still have one or two things to say. Time is running out.

What words can one use, though, that is the question. That is why I have been silent so far. Not silent exactly: after all, I'm a veteran lecturer by profession, a traveling lecturer for the Central Committee, a cultural worker. Which is to say, I use words a great deal. Nevertheless, there are still one or two things I must wrench forcibly out of silence. After all, I have seen the edge of the calm expanse.

I must state at the outset: I am an old lecturer, ridiculous even, and totally redundant—literally redundant, that is, redundant from every possible point of view. Often I disturb people by my very presence. For instance, when my work takes me into the Cultural Bureau or the Kibbutz Movement Head Office, even the typing girls immediately attack their machines, in case I engage them in conversation. That's how bad it is. All in all, I know, I am not easy to put up with.

I have no relationships. I don't mean by that relationships with women, though perhaps the word carries certain connotations; I haven't had any real relations with a woman since the days of the

Mandate. No, I'm using the word 'relationship' in its widest sense. I simply don't have any relationships. You see, when people speak to me I often don't hear, and when I myself am speaking other people hear little or nothing at all.

Even though by nature I am a great talker.

It is as if, let us say, I were a solitary sailor on a raft on the open sea. No other man, no seagulls, no wind, the current very gentle, even the water seems congealed. That's how I am, left all alone.

By the way, there is one thing I must make quite clear: the raft is falling apart. I shall soon be dead. I say this with complete equanimity, because to me death is something almost incidental, a clumsy accident, a kind of cheap effect. After all, I have seen the edge of the vast expanse.

Am I indifferent, then, to my own death? No, it's not a matter of indifference, but rather a kind of distance, a sort of screen which is very difficult to describe in words.

In any case, words, I always say, are a nasty business altogether. But on the other hand, shouting or laughter doesn't suit my temperament at all.

Perhaps I should enter into details a little. For ten years now the blood pressure has been dangerously erratic. I could die tomorrow. Two years ago a small growth was removed from my stomach, and my motions still entail hideous torture. And I'm a fat man, too, and getting fatter all the time, and I smoke one cigarette after another. All these things are destroying the body. I liken myself to the Jew in the joke, who sits calmly and smokes in a crashing airplane because the plane is not his property.

Sometimes at unexpected moments I can hear or sense a kind of swishing sound inside my head, like the hushed whishing of tires on a wet road: shshsh. While outside my graying hair is falling out. What's more, even on hot days I seem to be seized with shivers. So I am gradually disintegrating, but I don't let it trouble my mind. Na! After all, my mind is not disintegrating yet.

In the irritating event that one of the pains attacks me with unusual vigor, I keep a motley collection of pills and tablets that various doctors have prescribed over the years for various illnesses. I always carry a few packages in my jacket pockets. If a pain appears and insists on interrupting my work, I swallow a handful of pills indiscriminately. If they don't do the trick I swallow some more. In any case, it is always possible to baffle any pain by means of a few glasses of brandy.

Only drinking distracts my thoughts, and I am very concerned for my thoughts. Besides, there is the danger of ending up brandy-merry, which would be fundamentally opposed to my temperament, and consequently annoying.

Moreover, my teeth are decaying furiously. Or rather, not so much the teeth as the gums. I know that my breath smells. I always have to keep my distance. People are unable, do not even try, to conceal their disgust. After all, I myself feel disgust.

But I do not have the right yet to shut myself away or to depart. I still have one or two things left to say.

I live in a Party Workers' housing development. One room, kitchen, the usual facilities, a balcony, and a well-lit hall. Enough for my needs. Only the ceiling, for its part, is too low. And the walls let in the damp, or perhaps they produce it themselves, because even in summer gray flowers of damp blossom on them. Mildew is spreading in the corners. And what's more, the floor in my apartment insists on sloping toward the middle of the room: I have to put blocks under the legs of the table, otherwise even the tea in my glass would tend to slant slightly. And the periodic blocking of the drains is a degrading problem.

Hell, that's what always happens to me. Here I was, meaning to talk about great themes, to say something about national deliverance, and all of a sudden the sewage raises its head. Na! Is it any wonder that people recoil from me so disgustedly? Me, who once was so close to being elected to Parliament. However, that was many years ago, in the days of the first Constituent Assembly, in the year 1949.

In brief, during these damp suffocating summer nights I am making the acquaintance of my death.

I am far from panicking.

Rather, how shall I say, I am filled with disgust.

This death comes at night and tries to open the screen door between my room and the balcony. Over and over again he tugs at the handle, trying to open the door outward although it is made to open inward. Evidently he cannot claim much practical expertise. Finally he succeeds in opening the door and comes into the room, smelly, rotund, shortish, and not very clean, panting, too, and soaked in sour sweat. As for me, I lie there with my eyes wide open and watch him approaching. He sits down heavily on the foot of my bed and touches my feet through the sheet with his finger tips, in the same way as the old Health Service nurse, Huma Spielberg, touches me before she pushes the needle into me when I go for my twice-weekly injections. Oh yes, I forgot to mention that I also have to have some injections at regular intervals.

Now one final remark, before I move on to completely different subjects: when I am smoking, my own fingers seem strange to me, as if they were not my own. Someone else, someone disgusting, is suddenly holding my cigarette.

But, after all, soon I shall be beyond all these details, so why get involved in them for nothing. Instead of telling all about myself, would it not have been better to talk about others? A poet, say, or a national figure. Surely it would be perfectly possible to tell an engaging story about Moshe Dayan, for instance, the Minister of Defense, a young, energetic, and thoroughly attractive personality who is not lacking in charm. But Dayan has never taken the trouble to reply to the two letters I have written to him, and that is the reason we have so far never met. And so, despite myself, I am compelled to talk about myself instead of Dayan.

Here I am, sixty-eight years old, alone, neither loving nor loved. I feel I have been granted this last reprieve so that I can try to find a certain formula and put one or two things into words. And after that I shall give myself up without a struggle.

Well now, I don't know if I have mentioned my name: my name is Shraga Unger. I am a veteran traveling lecturer for the Central Committee. On Friday evenings I travel from kibbutz to kibbutz. Sometimes I am sent to a local Workers' Council for a Friday discussion or a question-and-answer session. I appear at seminars, one-day conferences, I take part in symposiums, study groups, workers' retreats, occasionally I even lecture before a gathering of Party activists.

My one and only subject is Russian Jewry. I am a monomaniac. I always keep half a dozen sets of lecture notes in my jacket pocket, all of them variations on the same theme. But the theme itself is a deep and awesome one.

From time to time I vary the title or single out a particular aspect: 'The Yiddish Language in the Soviet Union: A Plea for Help,' 'The Conspiracy of Silence—How Much Longer?' 'Our Brethren Under the Yoke of the Oppressor,' or 'Let My People Go.' I shall return to this theme presently. My path is mapped out; the silence of the vast expanse will be trapped in my net of words. The mighty river of the galaxies flows on night by night toward the soul of the universe, toward the edge of the splendor of the final void: surely together with everything else Russian Jewry is also swept along in its blazing silent flow.

Moreover, for many years I was accompanied in my travels by a middle-aged Trades Union singer, Liuba Kaganovskaya. We appeared together, she and I, all over the country. She read out documents, I gave my lecture, she sang songs, I summed up.

Over the years, Liuba Kaganovskaya's voice gradually cracked and gave out. She was given, I believe, some position with the Working Women's Council.

Since then I always travel alone.

I am sure you know the smell of the lonely roads at night, in Galilee, in the Jordan valley, in the western Negev. Sad and remote. You are driven from darkness to darkness in a dusty old truck by a hulking farm hand or a weary cultural worker. The headlight beams are foreign to the night fields, foreign even to themselves. Your speed rends the darkness, and it responds with a low howl. Occasionally a nocturnal animal crosses the desolate road, is trapped by the beam, bristles, and vanishes.

The brakes may squeal, and your head hits the windshield.

Then the silent wind and the smell of darkness. Sometimes you are suddenly gripped by a panic: the strange driver may attack and strangle you; the earth may rise up and fall on you; a star may drop down on you. Na! And so a blind wave of fervor boils up inside you and floods your soul, and you find yourself suddenly expecting an instantaneous illumination, a break in the clouds, something must, absolutely must reveal itself, a formula, a dazzling system, a purpose, surely it is inconceivable that you will go from birth to death without experiencing a single flash of illumination, without encountering a single ray of sharp light, without *something* happening, surely it is impossible that all your life you have been nothing more than a barren dream inside yourself, surely there is something, something must make itself known, there must be something....

But this expectation always dies away into the darkness, soon you are smoking a cigarette, and already you are coughing. Your stomach is troubling you. You feel the need to scratch yourself or to sneeze. And if for a moment a certain possibility existed, it has merely brushed past without really touching you.

Furthermore, that stranger sitting beside you in the driver's seat: he certainly did not hear your lecture, it was his turn to be the night driver and so he is driving at night, he is muffled and silent, much bigger and taller than you, can he have a thought of his own, what could you have to say to him in the night. Hand him one of your cigarettes, and offer him a light.

And so, as the engine gnaws its way through the mournful silence of the countryside, you sink deeper and deeper inside your weary self, and as you drive past Yavniel in the darkness for some reason you call it Novozibkov in your heart. And yet there is no need, no need whatsoever.

Incidentally, there was a time when I thought, I'll learn to drive myself, and travel from place to place under my own steam. I'll finish my lecture, take my leave of the audience and the chairman, sail away home or to the next kibbutz on my itinerary, no longer be a burden, change my whole life. And indeed some years ago I bought a copy of the rules of the road and set myself to studying them for two or three hours each day.

But after a while I ended up in despair; the whole idea was fundamentally unsuited to my temperament.

Chapter two

Now something is happening to me. They are trying to get rid of me. That is, the people who run the Cultural Bureau are in on the conspiracy. Perhaps they have had instructions from higher up. There are foreign agents everywhere, I know there are.

These long drives late at night to remote kibbutzim in outlying parts of the country are not good for me, they say, at my age. It's time for me to take a well-earned rest. They have had the idea of finding me a new position, either with the Central Committee or else in the Cultural Bureau.

Moreover, they say, I am not as young as I used to be. And the style I employ in my lectures, they say, that rumbustious style of mine, well, how to put it, the new generation needs to be addressed, it would appear, in a different sort of style. And then, I am such an extremist in the presentation of my subject, forever cursing the Bolsheviks, exaggerating things, they say. Wouldn't it be good for you, Comrade Unger, to take a rest. To relax both your efforts and your fury. Hand on the torch, as it were, peacefully to the next generation. You ought to take things easy.

You ought to take your rightful place in this building, the place your seniority and your achievements have earned you.

In short, Shraga, what should we say... some translating, perhaps, a bit of proofreading, stylistic editing—after all, Comrade Unger, you have such a fine stock of words, you know your Hebrew grammar, and you translate so beautifully from Russian, the great poet Shlonsky himself several times praised your work. You see, Shraga dear, we don't underestimate you. In this building you are one of the grand old men. There's not a single man here who could imagine doing without you, heaven forbid. All it boils down to, you see, is a kind of changing of the guard. Personalities come and go, but our mission continues. And we must take your health into account. We are none of us getting any younger. And the sad thing, my dearest Unger, is that times, as you know, are changing, there's an ill wind abroad in the country, and it's only very adaptable and practical-minded men perhaps who are able to win over the younger generation. Na! You'll surely agree to think it over for a day or two, a week or two even, and let us have your answer one way or the other.

That's how far things have gone.

Very well then: No.

I will not think it over. I won't give it a thought. Not for a moment. I shall stick to my post, I shall go on raising the alarm about the fate threatening Russian Jewry, and I shall not let the Bolsheviks off the hook. And as for this conspiracy, this sickening plot, I won't give them the slightest opportunity to silence me as well. It's out of the question. In fact it's even ugly. Literally ugly, that is, ugly from every possible point of view.

Nevertheless, they seem to think that I am going out of my mind. And for my own part, whenever I stand and stare, so to speak, from a great distance at the sea or the sand dunes or even, let's say, at the night sky, and when in my mind I compare these silent entities with all the possible words, I conclude the comparison with great caution and come to a positive decision: they are by no means exaggerating. I am indeed going out of my mind, though not in every sense of the word. But what of it. It is a slow, almost imperceptible process of changing perspectives. The seasons come and go.

Let me put a question to you, ladies and gentlemen, frankly and without any ulterior motive. Is there anything wrong with a change of perspective? No, I say, and again no. On the contrary. Lies, mental slavery, surely these are what is despicable. Whereas a change of perspective, on the other hand, qualifies as a private process which takes place within one's own soul.

In short, I stand fast. I have never denied or disguised the fact that I am ridiculous, obstinate, importunate, and, to cap it all, redundant. Redundant from every point of view. But I have never told a lie. Not I. In every debate, at every conference, I have always called a disgrace a disgrace and a wolf a wolf. I have never allowed myself to be silenced. That's how I am by nature, and I should like to have it in writing, signed and witnessed.

And now, comrades, to the principal point. That is to say, to my constant theme. The question of the Jews of Soviet Russia. The Bolshevik plot to exterminate the Jewish people as a first step toward the dismemberment of the whole world.

Under no circimstances will I cease to travel from kibbutz to kibbutz and from Jew to Jew, to sow the seeds of truth in every heart. The Bolsheviks have taken a secret decision, comrades, to put an end to the Jewish people once and for all. Nothing less, and perhaps even worse. I have no doubts, I even have evidence, which I shall not make public but will present personally to Moshe Dayan. So far they are content with terror, persecution, decrees, humiliation, and verbal abuse. But after all, that's exactly how Hitler began.

While we, for our part, what, I ask, are we doing?

Sleeping, comrades, sweetly sleeping.

Comrades, we must be raving mad. Consider: There, in the Kremlin, in the snow, the lights burn all night in the windows and the apparatchiks are sitting at their desks drinking endless glasses of tea all night long, and calmly drawing up plans for our slaughter. All scientific. All neatly filed by their secretaries.

And at such a time our people here play at diplomacy, send notes. Na! And we are supposed to be a clever race. We didn't even fathom Hitler in time. We didn't even begin. A whole flood of signs and warnings assailed us, and what did we do? Sent notes. Played diplomatics. And we said to ourselves: Nothing will happen, it's impossible.

Yet right now, at this very moment, the Bolsheviks at home and abroad are lulling us to sleep. Mesmerizing us. I put a simple question to you, comrades: Do you really think that all they are interested in is Yiddish newspapers? Do you think they will merely close a few down synagogues and stop at that? Since when is the bear content to munch a handful of nuts and then go quietly to sleep? No, comrades. All this is merely the hors d'oeuvres. Sharpening the knife. They are after our lives, comrades, after our very lives, literally. And it's not just the Jews of Russia they're after, it's us here in Israel as well. The Red fleet is splashing about in the Mediterranean, just around the corner. Coming to sniff us out. All of us at once. To kill the whole Jewish people at a single blow. One morning we'll all wake up and rub our eyes, and *snap*! comrades, the trap will be sprung and we will be caught.

I am convinced of this: it will all burst out at once, with co-ordination, with precision, everywhere. A massacre. In Byelorussia, in the Ukraine, in Tel Aviv, in the region of Kharkov, in the Jezreel valley, in the Asiatic Republics, in Moscow itself. And all according to a plan, a diagram. They are great experts on organization, and they know how to plan their massacres.

Comrades, I know these Bolsheviks; I know them through and through. I personally was not born a Social Zionist: originally I was a revolutionary, a real revolutionary, a revolutionary heart and soul. I was a Deputy Commissar over there in the year 1919. Regional Chairman. District Secretary in Viazma in 1921. I rose to the rank of Supervisor of the Miestkom. I even spent three or four hours once in Viazma with Zinoviev himself. We drank together, we joked, and on that occasion I actually cornered Zinoviev and forced him to cancel a project that was running into difficulties. Just imagine. As I was saying: I know the Bolsheviks by heart.

Now, with your permission, comrades, I shall return to my subject. At the very moment when the organized slaughter of citizens of Hebrew nationality begins all over Russia, there will be a simultaneous military onslaught on us here in Israel.

The Arabs, comrades, are only an excuse for them. A pretext. The crux of the matter is entirely different. They will suddenly turn up here with ships. And rockets. And airplanes. Maybe even atoms.

And so my contention is that we ought to get moving right away and do terrible things. Because as soon as the Bolsheviks have finished massacring us they will start destroying the whole world. Isn't that precisely the kernel of their ideology? In order to carry out their plan they may use gas, viruses even, bacteria, cosmonauts, other planets, sputniks, huge bombs hurled down from outer space: I was personally present at their secret meetings in the year 1919, and nobody knows better than I do what they are capable of. And they will begin, comrades, as they always do, with the Jews.

It is possible that in my zeal I exaggerate slightly. I do not deny it. But when it comes to the essence I am not exaggerating in the least. On the contrary. My perspective is very sharp. I am close to some kind of illumination. And they won't silence me.

And now, with your permission, I should like to touch upon one further aspect. I believe it will be the last.

Why is everybody in Israel silent?

Why are we not moving heaven and earth?

In other words, why do we not take preventive measures? We could take drastic steps, I say. Wait a moment. I shall give you the details at once. Let me follow my own course. I must proceed systematically from subject to subject. If we abandon logic what are we left with? Black chaos, that's what.

We all know what our people are doing. Saturday protest meetings, a symbolic empty chair at the Passover meal, complaints, human rights, diplomatics.

But let me ask you a simple question, comrades. Where is our espionage? Where are our detectives? After all, we have our own little fist now in Israel—all the goyim know that now. Our own secret services. Undercover agencies. Secret connections. That's what we ought to be using to stamp Bolshevism out now, before it's too late.

I declare, comrades, I declare with all the agony and fury in my heart, that there are traitors in our midst. Red agents scurrying everywhere. They have been carefully planted here. No, no orange juice, thank you, just plain tap water. Even Ben Gurion's confidential adviser was a Bolshevik in disguise until they caught him. They infiltrate everywhere. Every night Russian officers are stealing across our borders. Expert agitators are insinuating themselves into our internal organs. The Party, the authorities, the Central Committee. They may even be jumping on us out of airplanes under cover of night, in the Negev, the Judean Hills, the Dead Sea. And then suddenly there they are, strolling the streets of Tel Aviv in broad daylight, and no one can tell the difference. That's how they are undermining us from the inside. Some kind of Academy of Subversive Activities they've got there, in the depths of the forest, in the region of Krasnoyarsk, and it's there that they are trained for their missions.

Our submarines suddenly vanish at sea as if a circus juggler had hidden them up his sleeve. I know that juggler, comrades, I know him only too well. Perhaps that is why they have been undermining me personally as well recently. Trying to get rid of me or to silence me. They pretend to be worried about my health. But really they are plotting to shut me up with some sort of translating, because I am watching and can see it all. Between you and me, comrades, I for one am convinced that it is still not too late. We still have a chance of preventing the approaching catastrophe. Here is how: we must penetrate, and under perfect cover. What we must do is plant our own *agents provocateurs* in their midst; secretly and systematically plant Israeli agents inside the Sovnarkhoz, here and there infiltrate the Ispolkom, perhaps even the Comintern, the Supreme Soviet, the very Presidium itself.

In other words, a Jewish counterconspiracy.

Just that.

And then, I say, we must catch and poison them. Na! In times of danger no holds are barred. These Red perils, these murderers of the Jewish people must be poisoned. One by one. Literally poisoned. And before it's too late. After all, it's certainly not beyond our power. Let us take as our example that handful of heroic doctors, Jews like ourselves, who risked their very lives to poison the archmurderer Stalin himself with strychnine like a stray dog. And time, comrades, let us not forget time. Time is running out.

By the way, I must tell you that I have already tried my hardest. Last winter I wrote and even sent a detailed personal memorandum on this subject to Comrade Moshe Dayan. I presented him both with facts and with intuitions. I shall return to this point presently. I am determined to force Moshe Dayan to see the truth. But for the time being I go my own way. I refuse to be silenced.

Soon I shall have to die. Meanwhile I have been granted a reprieve so that I can try and say one or two things. But they are just the very things that I have never yet been able to put into words. And time, for its part, is moving on and on and on.

But what of it, say I. Inside the blazing river, inside this solar system which flows silently on through the darkness of the galaxy, my letter which I wrote to Moshe Dayan is being swept steadily on in the mighty soundless movement. The pages are yellowing, yes, I cannot deny that they are yellowing. Yet in my heart of hearts I know that these pages, like everything else, participate in the eternal flow. Not a single word will be lost.

I also intend to seek out Liuba Kaganovskaya. I have got to see her. Maybe she knows something. Perhaps without being aware of it she holds some small key. After all, Liuba traveled with me in all my wanderings over many years. She accompanied my lectures with musical interludes. Maybe she still remembers, maybe she hasn't forgotten. I have got to talk to her. Ask her. Persuade her. And after that I shall make my decision.

Finally, as so often happens to me, I suddenly descend into self-mockery. This outburst of emotion is absolutely absurd. The silent expanse accepts itself in silence. And I have seen the edge of the mighty expanse with my very eyes. The only thing that stands between me and it is the choice of the right words. But the raft, as I have already said, is falling apart.

Chapter three

Over the years I have contracted a number of bad habits. Vices. Some of them I detest, and yet I am unable to rid myself of them.

Take my daily routine, for instance.

I waste between three and five hours every day reading the newspapers. My apartment is snowed under with daily papers, weeklies, newsletters, periodicals, and leaflets of every kind. And the evening papers: on the coffee table, the kitchen table, piled high in the corridor, in the throne room, and around my bed, under my bed, inside my bed. I am besieged in my own apartment by a regular army of old newspapers.

Sometimes I resolve to fight back. One fine morning I leap out of bed full of energy, I furiously arrange them all in piles and tie them up carefully with string, and then I literally sit down to wait for the Boy Scouts to come and do their duty by taking my treasures away.

What nonsense. Those Boy Scouts will never turn up. Young people nowadays spend their time laughing, playing games—what do they care about old newspapers?

As for the newspapers themselves, they soon untie themselves and settle down again all over the place.

So time, my time, is steadily trickling away. I cannot break myself of the habit of reading the papers. There are so many things I thirst to find out about: border violations, confrontations of rival ideological systems, political intrigues, signs from outer space, a sort of anarchist conference the other day in Brussels where an executive committee was elected by a large majority.

Surely some of these things are capable of provoking powerful reactions. These days even the simplest events seem to boil over, signs and omens simmering everywhere.

Take Berl Locker, for instance, the veteran Zionist leader. He addresses a congress of youth workers from all over the Jewish diaspora. And I spend half the morning sitting in my room putting my comments down on paper one by one. What benefit is there, I ask myself, in these comments of mine? Surely even Berl Locker himself has completely forgotten his speech by now. No, I answer, there is no benefit for anybody. Well, I say, what of it if there is no benefit? Even the stars and planets in the galaxy revolve regularly without bringing any benefit. Nothing is in vain. Everything lasts forever. The slightest action or gesture cannot be taken back. Not a grain of sand will ever be lost. What does it mean to be lost? It is nonsense, utter nonsense, to talk like this. Can something which exists suddenly become nothing? Can anything ever escape from the universe? Certainly not. Everything is confined within itself. Totally confined. Confined forever.

Let us suppose I manage to capture a thought in words, and put it down on paper. What follows? The thought will be imprisoned in words, and won't be able to escape. A minor event has occurred, and it can never be taken back.

By strict observation, therefore, I say, one can establish a rule: every event is momentous.

Besides the newspapers, I have a constant relationship with the radio. In the course of the day I listen to five, six, or eight news broadcasts. Sometimes wild things happen which throw the mind into a turmoil. Certain events even seem to challenge the very laws of nature.

For instance, early in the morning the girl declares with conviction: Later this month Abdul Nasser is to go to Moscow to request modern armaments. Fomenting some new political intrigue.

Later on, however, at lunchtime, the girl is sent packing with all due respect, and a male announcer takes her place with something entirely different: The announcement of Abdul Nasser's impending visit to Moscow is described as premature. As yet it has received no official confirmation.

In the course of the afternoon news bulletin on the commercial network there is a further announcement on the same subject: it is the Egyptian War Minister who will head the delegation to Moscow. Na! Someone completely different.

Finally, late at night, the whole story is turned on its head. The Egyptians are not going to see the Russians, but, on the contrary, vice versa: a special delegation from the Kremlin is on its way to Cairo. As if the arrogant girl in the morning had invented the whole thing out of her own head. This very morning, while she was bombarding us with her proclamations, this Red delegation was already buzzing over the Black Sea on its way to Cairo.

That's how bad things are.

At this point I must explain something carefully. It is not the prestige I care about. I don't give a fig whether Ivan goes to see Mohammed or Mohammed pays a visit to Ivan. It's all one to me. The nub of the matter is this: what fascinates me is the reversal of the order. For a brief moment the beams of light fall from odd angles and produce an astonishing combination, a fantastic configuration, the sequence of time flows backward for an instant and suddenly splits up into several nervous interweaving currents, sooner has become later and the last has become first. What in the morning was undisputed truth has become a hollow lie by evening, as if the most elementary and unchallengeable laws of nature have undergone a second's hesitation.

And if I only listened to one or two broadcasts a day I could have missed the whole experience completely.

In short, I am a receptive man, I read a great deal, and my mind is full of all kinds of strange thoughts. And in between the thoughts there comes an occasional sudden, how shall I call it, intuition.

Another habit I have: on those evenings when I am not traveling I lie in my bed reading the works of the early Zionists until one or two o'clock in the morning. The fathers of the Jewish Labor Movement were remarkable men. I could browse in their writings for hours on end. If only we held fast to the light of their vision, I say, we might be able to spare ourselves something of the disaster in store for us. We have had a prior warning from the founding fathers of the Movement, but we have been deaf to it.

And so, draped in a sheet, my balding head propped up on three or four large pillows, the fading bedside lamp casting its light on my thoughts and my nocturnal silence, I plow my way through the pages.

Shadows revolve round the corners of the room. They seem to be trying to burrow their way into the depths. The ideas I encounter in the books are kind to me, like a distant melody playing to me in the night.

You probably know the feel of these summer nights here in Tel Aviv. The sea filters in through the moldering shutters and blows its tepid sweaty breath in your face. Sourly your death comes in and sits panting for a minute or two on the foot of your bed. Afterward you may hear the swish of tires on the dark asphalt. A faraway shout. A telephone ringing in another apartment.

All these sounds, I say, mount up at night into a grim threat.

And suddenly vast steppes, empty gray steppes call out to you again and again. Call out to you with a terrible peace. Shraga. Listen.

Yes. Here I am. Listening.

Listen.

And silence.

The desperate shout in the middle of the night or the distant telephone ringing in the small hours may be marking a turning point in somebody's life. Maybe a woman has run away, or the secret service has discovered something, killed a traitor, or a neighbor may have had a revelation in a dream. Everything in Tel Aviv, on these sinister, suffocating nights, is open to several interpretations.

Every night sounds of laughter come from the balcony opposite. They play cards there all night long, tearing cheese straws, chomping peanuts, joking in Polish. What, I wonder, can make those people so cheerful.

As if words could really still be used like that. Joking in Polish. Na!

One night I got out of bed at three o'clock in the morning, dressed hurriedly, lit a furious cigarette. I was intending to go out on the balcony and scold them until I scared them into silence. But I could not find the right words to warn them forcefully enough against their use of words. And shouting or laughter, as I have already said, does not suit my temperament. So I got undressed and angrily climbed back under my sheet. Then I had to get out of bed again because I had left my cigarette butt burning on the edge of the ashtray. How foolish.

I should like to say this: The sea begins two or three blocks away. It crouches there in the darkness, steaming. Do those cheerful neighbors of mine spare a thought for the sea's purpose? Such a seething mass growling and panting at us out there in the darkness. Its very dimensions are demented, almost malicious.

The sea itself seems to be illuminated from within in places by a black light. It is the light of night and I know how amazingly gentle it is. When the moon comes out and touches these patches of black inner light with its silvery rays, the sea depths seem to arch and curve up slowly in longing, with powerful silent patience.

It is a phenomenon menacing enough, I say, to make your flesh creep.

In my mind's eye I can see almost tangibly the seething depths of the sea, the hush of inner rage against the wake drawn on the waves by the movement of forces patrolling backward and forward in the darkness.

The interplay between the engines and the fury of the quiet water in the night is serious, deadly serious.

Still, we must not forget the submarine Dakar. We dare not forget her. It is not impossible that she is still drifting, abandoned, unlighted, in the underwater currents, carried from place to place, at the mercy of powerful forces such as a man may encounter only in his dreams or in the throes of death. Her crew must have been long since taken off to a secret prison camp on the furthest edge of the vast plains of Baikonor, beyond the forests of Karaganda. While the submarine *Dakar* is abandoned to the shifting water, unmanned, unlighted, and the panting tide toys with her rusting hull.

I know that the tide is not an independent force, but merely the submission of the water to the movement of the moon in its orbit. And this orbit in its turn is subject to other orbits which are mightier far than it. And so the whole universe is held fast in the circling grip of strong bands, the forces of Earth and Sun, planets and comets, the galaxies, blindly erupting forces ceaselessly stirring the ripples of silence to the very depths of black space.

All these entities, you know, are not easy to descry from Tel Aviv. But I have caught a glimpse of them myself once or twice, at night. From here.

It goes without saying that I find it very difficult to get up in the morning.

To get up; certainly not to wake up.

There is nothing difficult about waking up. I am a very light sleeper. The milkman cycles along my street, the lover of the divorcee next door starts his car, and already I am wide awake. So uncertain is my sleep. On the other hand, my waking hours are also slow and halfhearted. I open my eyes, my lips say to me, Get up, get up, but get up is precisely what I am unable to do. On the contrary, in these moments of waking up I am assailed by all kinds of tortured hallucinations. Many years ago I had a cat here. I used to call her Krasavitsa, I used to stroke her. She, for her part, enjoyed playing with my shoelaces. It was all a long time ago. My Krasavitsa died when Golda Myerson was still our ambassador in Soviet Russia. But sometimes when I wake up in the morning I start vividly imagining that the cat is lying in my bed as usual, resting on my stomach, purring contentedly in her sleep.

And then I fall prey to hideous torments.

I find it hard to believe myself, but it is a fact. I suddenly feel stirrings of desire. In my body, that is. It stirs ruthlessly, brazenly, desperately.

I, who stopped looking at women altogether many years ago. I, who am hardly able to say the simplest thing to a woman. For instance, when my work takes me into the Cultural Bureau or the Kibbutz Movement Head Office, even the typing girls immediately attack their machines.

There's nothing for it. How can one argue with this force. The torture attacks me, seizes me from all sides at once, brutally shakes my whole body, humiliates me utterly. And all for no reason.

The imagination starts inventing combinations. A shapely waist appears, and immediately I am on fire. An undraped shoulder. Other private parts. Gentle, half-remembered curves. Various titillating lines.

But soon my imagination stumbles on a shaming obstacle: time and distance distort the picture. A violent disruption shatters the sequence ordained by nature. I mean, it suddenly seems to me for some reason as if the physical act between the sexes is simply not feasible. Geometrically impossible. As if precluded by one's very physiology. And at that point the torture becomes almost too much for me to bear.

And the degradation.

How ridiculous it all is. If I could only stand aside and watch, I should probably burst out laughing. And yet how desperate. Are there any words to describe it?

Sometimes a kind of relief comes to me afterward. As if the carnal desire has yielded despite itself.

A nervous calm descends on me.

I lie back in bed with my eyes open. Heartburn eats at my innards.

My glance wanders vaguely over the low ceiling. The photograph of the labor leader Berl Katznelson on the wall opposite. A map of the settlements of our land. A pair of metal chairs. And all the old newspapers. An open magazine with its yellowing cover uppermost at the foot of the bed. Cigarette butts. My slippers. A twisted corpse stretched full-length on the floor in the half-darkness. My trousers. The gray shape of the wastepaper basket between the legs of the desk. More cigarette butts.

I close my eyes.

My thoughts still seek out the presence of a woman, any woman. I ask for so little. Less than the brush of a pair of lips, or even a caress. Just some kind of touch without the shadow of an ulterior purpose: a woman's hand straightening my collar and accidentally touching the back of my neck. A woman's hand gently removing a stray hair from my chin, almost without her noticing what she has done to me. Like that. In the course of conversation. A stray hair from my chin. Or some girl coming up to me in the street to pin a flag to my lapel.

I ask for so little. It occurs to me that, just as one has a civil right to breathe the air or express an opinion, so every citizen ought to have the right to touch with his finger tips, and occasionally to be touched by someone else. And the right should extend even to dilapidated old citizens. It is a terrible thing to live like this for years and years without ever touching or being touched. Even by accident. Is it anything indecent I am asking?

Even so, I find myself so obscene that I want to gnash my teeth.

There are so many possible women. The switchboard operator at the Head Office. The divorcee next door. Perhaps even Liuba. Or one of the cleaning women. The secretary of the Working Mothers' League. The grocer's wife.

I feel like a beggar. Like an old stray dog.

I, who am ashamed to even sit next to a woman on a public bus.

Finally, as always, I rise to a generalization: What a distance, I say, what a distance looms between people. Between men and women. Between Jews. Between people who share an ideology, a party, a way of life. What a distance, what a dark distance, whole galaxies of distance separate every man from every other man. Dread takes hold of me.

At about five to seven every morning the divorcee next door goes out. Her lover has left an hour earlier, coughing heavily. Now she herself goes out, with a popular tune on her lips.

She slams her door, and at the sound I always push myself out of bed and grope my way into my trousers. While one hand feels for the buttons, the other is already reaching out to the radio: the seven o'clock news.

Chapter four

The reprieve which has been granted me to try to touch the edge of things with words is running out, expiring. And even in the outside world something is pulsing with dread, so that dim drumbeats seem to accompany the announcer's voice on the seven o'clock news. A desperate prolonged strain, a pressure built up almost beyond breaking point, is about to burst with furious violence. The Warsaw Pact forces are mustering and advancing by various routes, over hills and through forests, toward the great Summer Maneuvers beneath the Carpathian mountains. In Berlin secret documents have disappeared without a trace. Obstinate rumors are circulating that the Bolsheviks plan to fire some gigantic rocket into outer space soon, with an unknown objective.

And you, are you capable of catching the nuances? Of sensing the suppressed eruption which is bubbling underneath these events? The sands of time seem to be running out. Even the easterly wind, for instance, which blows on Tel Aviv from the mountains, betrays a sudden hesitation. One moment it dies down, and the next it ruffles the dry oleander bush in the garden, then it has faded and gone. So it was nothing but a flicker. A final spasm.

I concentrate hard on the act of shaving in the morning, in case the razor nicks my face. The folds of skin make shaving very difficult. There is always a slight smell of damp in the bathroom, no matter how well I air it. And the wet towel wafts the smell of my body nauseatingly back. Even the soap has a tendency to become slimy.

Then I pad barefoot into the kitchen. I make myself a glass of tea. In front of me on the kitchen table, besides the muddle of old newspapers, there is a scattering of cookie crumbs. And the dregs of last night's tea in a dirty glass. The lid of the jam jar has long since vanished, and an idiot fly has singled out the jar as a fitting place in which to commit suicide.

The sun, for its part, tortures my tired eyes through the east-facing window with its merciless rays. Sun, I say, with all due respect, what do you hope to find here? This said, I suit action to words: I stride across to the window and slam the shutters closed as if to shut out the night instead of the daylight. And the shutters? They squeak hideously, sending shivers down my spine.

Bread and margarine. Jam. Sour cream. A tomato which has gone horribly soft in the heat of the easterly wind. A glass of tea. Perhaps a second glass. Put the dishes in the sink, or lazily leave them where they are. The tap drips absent-mindedly. I wrestle with it till my fingers ache, but still it insists on dripping.

Then a cigarette. The matches, I ask with mounting anger, where are the matches?

Eight o'clock. Tel Aviv is already boiling and steaming. As if the very buildings will soon evaporate in the heat. Before we built a city on this spot the sand dunes stretched right down to the beach. The desert touched the sea. In other words, we came here and forced these two furious elements asunder. As if we poked our heads into the jaws of the sea and the desert There are moments on hot summer days when I have a sudden feeling that the jaws are trying to snap shut again. On us. The whole city suddenly seems to me almost unbelievably insubstantial. Even the trees we have planted along the edges of the pavements appear hardly to be joined to the ground. More like a stage set than a city. Nothing but a cardboard facade dividing the desert from the sea. One heavy Russian winter snowstorm, I say, could wipe Tel Aviv completely off the face of the earth. And my heart contracts at the thought. We are so fragile, all this is so impermanent.

They will appear suddenly out of the ground. Or out of the blue.

And the sea, for its part, crouches beneath the city, silently menacing.

The breath of the desert in our face.

The hateful sun.

The heat depresses me. Sweat breaks from every pore. I would take my shirt off, if it were not for the effort. I am a fat man, if you will excuse me, and getting fatter all the time. And redundant, totally redundant, redundant from every point of view.

Ah, at last the newspaper is pushed under the door, and I have to bend down to pick it up. Then I drag myself to my room. I sit down and breathe out heavily. I miss most of the eight o'clock news because my old radio warms up so slowly, almost as if it were doing it on purpose. The weather forecast: the highlands will be very dry and the humidity on the coastal plain will increase. Na! So for once I was right. What is the point, I wonder.

Is it really possible for a man to go on and on living pointlessly until at a random moment he finishes living and dies as if nothing?

A smell of roasting creeps in from outside. The whole city is baking in the sun, or maybe the Polish neighbors are cooking up some heavy meat stew again.

Who is this coming to see me in the morning? The electricity-meter reader has come and gone away again. Wait a moment, comrade meter reader, please, I have something to explain to you. Have you never heard the name Zinoviev?

What do the headlines in the newspaper say? Syria has decided to send an angrily worded complaint to U Thant. The roof of a housing development in Givat Olga has fallen in and two people have been buried alive. The crusading columnist Yehuda Gotthelf has once again denounced the hypocrisy of the bourgeois press.

I remember Olga. It was a long time ago. Far away, through a screen of sadness, beyond the flickering twilight, Olga. Olga Borisovna. At the end of Tyelega Lane. A bitter, vague landscape. Gray snow in the soft light of sunset. Wheel marks in the snow. A smell of flour. The smell of horses. Her face framed by her headscarf. Her tears. Her low warm laughter through the tears. Round about, in the corners of the courtyard, loose heaps of boxes and crates. The white forest like a caress on the slopes of the white hills. The taste of the wind. The frost. Her soft voice kissing every word. My heart flutters, more like a sick bird than a heart. Olga. Her legs lost inside a huge pair of men's boots. When she laughs her teeth show—tiny, white, and sharp. The freckles run riot on her cheeks as if endowed with a life of their own. The skin of her hands. Her fingernails broken by rough work. Her one-armed brother Osip, who refused to call me Shraga and leered as he addressed me as Sergei Moyseyevich. Olga and her brother with me in my basement room, Osip curled up in the corner playing a melancholy tune while she paints the walls, suddenly pulls my hair, her lips half-open and silent. Olga wrapped in a green shawl, peeling potatoes, trying in vain to burn damp logs, laughing: *Propadt, syriye drova, shtob ty propal.**

Her death.

My wanderings.

The gradual lonely decay of the body.

I feel like making my own angry complaint, just like the Syrian government. I feel grumpy today, I feel deprived, as usual. The floor is sinking, slowly and steadily, toward the center of the room. Hidden Bolsheviks are trying to remove me from my job so as to silence me. The plaster on the walls is turning yellow and peeling. My hair, in its turn, is going gray and falling out. I shall write another letter of complaint to Moshe Dayan, but this time I shall deliver it to him personally. I shall catch him on a street corner and block his path, I

* Russian: "Damn you, damp wood, damnation take you."

shall manhandle him into a back yard, I shall speak to him, I shall alert him, I shall alarm him, Comrade Dayan, please listen to me.

By the way, Yehuda Gotthelf, too, in his article about the bourgeois press, omitted two or three aspects of the question, as if deliberately to annoy. I tear a page out of my notebook and fill the gaps carefully and systematically.

Eleven o'clock. Heaven and earth blaze in the sun. Tel Aviv suffocates. Beneath the city the sea waits, and in the meantime flashes with smothered hatred. Various longings come upon me and are immediately stifled from within. There is something fundamentally false, I say, something vicious in the relationship between the temperature and the humidity.

The midday news. In Jerusalem, a top-level consultation. Andrei Gromyko has once again run riot and publicly abused the Jewish people. My stomach aches. Two tablets. A dead bird on the balcony. A big black cat appears, sniffs, puts out a paw, prods in disgust, and in disgust turns and disappears slowly among the dry oleander bushes in the garden. What a revolting cat. I have stirrings of hostility toward it.

Propadi.

At a quarter past one I leave the house. There is a cheap co-opera-tive restaurant on the corner of my street, and it is there that I take my midday meal. On my way out of the building I pause in the entrance hall. I root in vain in my letter box. In the restaurant I am attacked by hordes of furious flies. While I eat I run my eyes over the headlines in the evening paper, while I fan myself and drive off the flies with the morning edition. When I come to drink my tea I ring the changes, glancing at the morning paper and brandishing the evening one aloft. What blindness, I say, what pathetic blindness everywhere. If I were not so afraid of hyperbole, I would add: tragic blindness.

After my meal I make my way home. A cold shower. As usual the smell of my body wafts back at me nauseatingly from the towel. And yet in my youth I was consumed by an enormous enthusiasm, at times I was completely on fire with a wild joy, as if the whole Revolution were blazing away inside my chest.

How remote.

At a quarter to four a truck will come from the Central Committee to take me to Kibbutz Tel Yosef. Here it is, honking under my window. Why do you have to honk so, comrade driver? Do you really expect me to leap down the steps like a gazelle?

And then hours of traveling in the sun-baked driver's cab, with the stench of gasoline fumes, past gray or yellow fields, mercilessly scorched by the summer.

Is this how I should be using my reprieve? After all, this reprieve is final. This evening I shall lecture to the veteran settlers of Tel Yosef. I shall hammer on their chests with my old fists. They must understand and take fright before it is too late. Catastrophe is hanging over us all.

I have not forgotten. No, I follow my own orbit, my own order, my own rhythm, and even if my strength is failing, at least the wheels of the truck are full of life. They speed over the melting asphalt with a resolute rhythmic caress.

The earth, too, revolves in its orbit. And the sun. The whole galaxy either draws or is drawn. These laws never wear out. The Bolsheviks, however, are plotting to subvert this eternal motion, and their power is by no means negligible. Those Bolsheviks, I know them backward. And I shall not let go of them. I shall dig my rotting teeth into their tail with all my might and main.

I am being called.

Chapter five

Y ou must be familiar with the flavor of that sad feeling, of arriving at sunset, unknown and tired, in an old established kibbutz: the smell of newly mown lawns, the quiet music of calmly revolving sprinklers, the sound of showers, men in vests relaxing on deck chairs reading the newspaper, a group of children hurrying past you laughing, the evening breeze's caress, your loneliness.

A thin middle-aged Cultural Officer greets you earnestly but guardedly. He offers you a glass of chilled fruit juice. He invites you to take a shower to wash off the dust of your journey. Afterward he thrusts the kibbutz newsletter into your hands while his wife serves coffee and cake. And you, no matter how accustomed you are to traveling, are always at a loss. You are afraid you are putting them to trouble. Faintly you mumble unnecessary apologies. Over and over again you mutter: thank you, thank you, no need, really, thank you.

His wife or children may suddenly ask after your wife and children. You deny, defend yourself, as though charged with some kind of indecency. And as you talk you smile a dead smile.

Eventually a neighbor may come in. Someone who knows someone in the Cultural Bureau. He will sit down and join in the dragging conversation as if sniffing you out. He has heard your name before, of course. He can't recall where. You, in turn, offer round your city cigarettes. They start talking local politics, but soon move on to world problems. Tea is served.

You confine yourself to generalities; you take care to give them no hint of what is to come. You guard the secret of your mission jealously.

What is more, there is going to be a match of some kind this evening at Tel Yosef. They break the news to you in advance, so that you will not be disappointed by the absence of the young people from your lecture. The youth nowadays are carried away by basketballs; they lose no sleep over anti-Semitic manifestations in the Soviet State. Not that I blame them: after all, did I come here to address the youth? No, it is my own generation I have come to shake up. The younger generation move, I know, at a different pace. They run and dance, the younger generation, they play games After all, we have tried our hardest to raise up a tough, straightforward generation here in our land. As if we were trying to straighten out once and for all some kind of mental kink. So what right, I ask, do we have to be taken aback at the sight of a Jewish muzhik?

After supper they leave you alone. Alone on a small veranda, surrounded by flowerpots, in a comfortable armchair. You must want to relax and prepare yourself for your lecture. Na! And they have business of their own to take care of.

And so, vacant and weary, you sit and stare silently at the fading of day. A soundless blaze wounds the western horizon. The breeze conspires in whispers with the darkening treetops. A stubborn Russian verse by Lermontov or perhaps a stray line of Mayakovsky takes a relentless hold of you. As if the words had teeth, which had closed on your flesh.

All the dividing lines in the world outside gradually fade and merge. A kind of dark panting massivity closes slowly all around you. The shadows toss and turn heavily. There is no peace among the shadows, and no compromise between them and the solid objects.

Slight sounds come and go in the distance as if they were feeling the surface of the silence with wonderfully gentle fingers. Their great love makes them careful, very careful, not to hurt the silence.

Then the lights come on one by one in the small window frames. A curtain is drawn. A woman laughs. A motor starts rumbling in the distance.

This place is foreign to me.

All of a sudden the mooing of cows comes to you dimly out of the darkness like a stab of pain which releases a crumbling dam in the depths of your soul. At once the torment overflows. Your soul begins to writhe, haunted by sorrow and longing, to writhe like a body.

The blind might of the darkening lawns lies heavy upon you. In vain you close your eyes: beyond your shuttered eyelids the lawns grow ever darker. As if not here, not in the summer, but somewhere far away. The hot dry night falling around you gradually turns in your mind into black snow. The black snow falls on you, soft and sinister: someone is waiting for you. Shraga. Listen. Come. At once.

Where. How.

Beyond the farthest edge of the plains, beyond the dark forest, beyond the taiga, the tundra stretches right up to the limit of the glacier wall.

Someone is waiting for you. Come. Now. Your time is running out. Get moving. Shraga. Come on.

Na! Leave me. Do you think I am really capable of going?

I don't even feel confident. Perhaps it is a fraud. I won't budge. Once I was caught by a gigantic fraud, robbed of all my youth, I won't allow myself to be caught a second time. I'm not moving.

Do you really think I am capable of moving? I am only capable of swallowing a pill. Or possibly lighting a cigarette, stopping my ears. Huddling in silence.

At a quarter past nine they come and take me to the dining hall. I take a quick count. Eleven sleepy old men with sunken lips. Six old women. The Cultural Officer. Ashtrays scattered around the recently washed and disinfected dining tables. The knitting needles flash and sparkle in the hands of the old women. And Yosef Trumpeldor, the hero, stares down tight-lipped at me from his frame in his splendid uniform from the Russo-Japanese War.

I am introduced. Welcomed warmly. The light in the hall seems yellow, almost pinched. I rise to my feet. At the same moment a knitting needle falls clanging on the floor. You're on. Speak to the Children of Israel and they will hearken.

I commence with self-restraint. I begin by drawing the distinction between official and popular anti-Semitism in Russia.

The bureaucracy, I say, is conducting its anti-Jewish campaign in a cool and calculating manner. In exactly the same way as they organize, say, a gigantic industrial conglomerate. For the Red regime this sickening campaign has the character of an absolute necessity: as soon as the counterrevolution, real or imagined, ceases to simmer, the revolution itself will perish. That is the basis of dialectics. Therefore the Jews have been singled out to represent to the simpler folk an inflated bogeyman of a false counterrevolution. So much for the theoretical side. From here on they put the idea into practice: a specially trained professional team is ruthlessly set in motion, a secret branch of the Sovinform Bureau or the Theoretical Reindoctrination Institute is formed; all night long they drink strong tea and fabricate imaginary subversive activities by venal Jewish elements which have never existed. Who knows this technique better than I do. I know it personally, from the inside. From the year 1919. And in all these institutions the typing girls sit on their fat behinds copying and recopying the filth on their typewriters: accusations of all kinds against Jewish speculators, smuggling networks woven in secret by the cunning Jews, insidious counter revolutionary propaganda, dark plottings of the Joint Distribution Committee or international Zionism, a subtle conspiracy being fomented behind the curtain of every out-of-the-way synagogue. That is the sort of stew they are concocting, comrades, and serving up every morning through the press at the breakfast tables of the working masses. And all with the sole purpose of instilling fear into the minds of simple folk.

And now, comrades, permit me to depart from my subject for a moment so as to return to it immediately with renewed vigor. I wish to say something, ladies and gentlemen, about the famous Greek scholar Archimedes. This ancient sage was always in the habit of declaring: Just let me have a place to lever from, and I, for my part, will roll the whole earth effortlessly hither and thither. I believe there is still a measure of disagreement among the experts whether this man Archimedes was exaggerating or not. Everyone agrees, however, comrades, that in every generation anti-Semitism has served as a lever for tyrants who were egged on by the Devil himself to start pushing the whole earth hither and thither with their little fingers.

This is the sting, the central kernel of the matter. The Bolsheviks, I say, have chosen anti-Semitism as the lever to bring about the expansion of Red regimes all over the world, and if they achieve this aim, heaven forbid! they will not be satisfied with that but will start tampering with the rules of the universe, and try to throw the eternal order into turmoil.

What conclusions do I draw? The Jewish people, I say, must at last wake up and establish a sort of world shadow government, the same kind of terrible sinister conspiracy as our worst enemies credit us with. That way we shall strengthen ourselves and at the same time sow panic among our foes. Surely we ought to defend ourselves with the utmost vigor.

But, with your permission, I shall not dwell on this point. I go my own way. I set great store by order and method. I want to return at once to the theme of anti-Semitism, this time under a different aspect.

You are all familiar with the old type of anti-Semitism, the warmhearted anti-Semitism which is so widespread among the Russian masses. A picturesque form of anti-Semitism, I say, in its way, and in a certain sense almost endearing.

Imagine, comrades: Russia, a gigantic land of plains stretching on and on forever, and beyond the plains yet more plains, mountains, forests, steppes, mighty rivers, wastelands of eternal snow. It is only natural that, confronted by such an expanse, the Russian soul should be gnawed by overmastering sadness. The dread of immensity has the power to drive a man mad.

For generations upon generations the Slavic soul has been schooled in vicissitudes, torn between submission and savagery. The ignorant peasants are prey to unbelievable cruelty, especially when the cold tears their flesh with its vicious teeth. A Russian peasant is capable of standing up one fine day, slitting his own mother's throat and letting her bleed to death. And why should Vasily kill his own mother like this? Let us say, because his old father is maddened by a desire to marry some young peasant girl, and the old woman refuses to die. Vasily is miserable, he weeps to see his poor old father, unable to marry the girl, drowning his sorrows day by day in drink. And so one fine day Vasily ups and butchers the old woman to clear the way. And what is the moral, comrades: it was out of compassion that Vasily killed her. He could not contain his compassion. His heart was breaking with compassion and sorrow. But a month later, outside the village church, in the midst of the festivities for his father's marriage to the peasant girl, this same Vasily, after drinking like a madman, shatters the empty bottle over his father's head with his own hands and drowns the young bride in the river, because he is suddenly overcome with compassion for his poor dead mother.

And in the end, comrades, Vasily bursts out crying. He weeps hot tears. For twenty days and twenty nights he does not stop sobbing. And as he cries he tears his very soul to shreds with his fingernails.

There is no other country in the whole world, comrades, where tears flow in such floods. In Russia everybody weeps. Anyushka weeps because Vanya won't fall in love with her, and the next day she weeps again because he has changed his mind and suddenly fallen in love with her. Poets weep and agronomists weep. The working classes weep. The students weep. The cosmonauts weep from loneliness up among the stars. Even the secret police weep in secret. They subject their suspect to horrible tortures, they torture him to death, and then what? They weep, comrades, and how they weep!

Take me myself, for instance: I was imprisoned in the east of Smolensk in the year '23, because the newspapers said that a certain German Jew named Mungert had founded a Menshevik cell in Vienna.

You admit, Comrade Unger, the investigator said to me, you admit, do you not, that you are that villain's brother. Comrade Investigator, I said, I am my poor parents' only son. What is more, my name is Unger, not Mungert. What is more, in the year '19 the *Red Star* published a violently critical article of mine against the Mensheviks. But the investigator insisted: Comrade Unger, you are not telling me the truth and you cannot even look me straight in the face. If you continue to refuse to cooperate, Comrade Unger, we shall be forced to send you for special investigation.

In short, both of us held our ground, until finally he lost his temper. There was a glass of boiling hot tea on his desk, and in frustration or fury he seized it and dashed it in my face. At that point, comrades, my eyes filled with tears. And all of a sudden unmistakably similar tears appeared in his eyes, too. Na! And so for a while the two of us wept together like a pair of long-lost brothers. And then the investigation was resumed. As if nothing had happened. We both held our ground.

I am not exaggerating.

Can you imagine, comrades, the depth of this melancholy? As I have just said: Russians weep everywhere. Even the bandits in the salt mines weep, from savagery and sorrow.

A great nation. A wonderful nation.

Savagery and sorrow, I say, throughout the length and breadth of Russia. And they have had years and years of famine, plague, cold, norms, filth, drunkenness, lice, rags... and everywhere the same crazy combination of callous cruelty and savage compassion. All this is bound, absolutely bound I say, to burst out violently. Like the rivers flooding with the melting of the snow. And throughout the length and breadth of Russia, from Carpathorussia across the Urals to Siberia. In the primeval forests. On the steppes. On the tundra. In the Crimean War. In the Red Guard. In Budyonny's galloping cavalry. In God-forsaken villages. Everywhere the Russian soul is torn between savagery and submission.

And now, ladies and gentlemen, back to the main point: anti-Semitism. Imagine the scene: Dimitri is walking down the alley beside the synagogue, taking a casual evening stroll, tousled, whistling a cheerful tune, with no malice aforethought. He takes a peep through the window and sees inside the synagogue little human figures swaying fervently backward and forward. His ears catch a kind of low, long-drawn-out wailing. He halts. He stops whistling. Mitya, comrades, is overcome by compassion. Lonely souls like these, he feels, should really not be allowed to eat their hearts out like this for no good reason, as if this were the Wailing Wall in Palestine instead of Gogol Street in Moscow. Not to mention their perpetual speculation with the blood and fat of Mother Russia.

How can Mitya silence the demon sobbing inside his own heart?

And so, comrades, Mitya suddenly bends down, picks up a stone in the dark, weighs it angrily in his hand, muttering all the time, glances round him and—crash!—hurls it through the window. Na! Then he runs away, his heart overflowing with joy and sorrow.

That's how it is.

For a long time, ladies and gentlemen, I have held insistently to the following theory: the Jews in Russia are persecuted, they are persecuted viciously and savagely, but not without compassion. On the contrary. They are humiliated, but they are pitied. They try to stamp the Jewish people out root and branch, but at once their hearts burst out crying.

And why, I ask, have they built a dual carriageway over Babi Yar? Why did they kill the Jewish poets? Why have they been trying so hard to wipe us out all these years? Because they are afraid, I say. They are frightened that a warm blind national sentiment will suddenly well up inside them and sweep everything away, Jewish Section, Central Committee, dialectical method, and all. In short, the whole Revolution there hangs by a thread. It was created by Jews and it can be destroyed by Jews.

Such a great nation. Such a miserable nation. They tear us apart with their claws, only to get up the next morning and drown in an ocean of agony, remorse, and compassion. They must suffer from a kind of longing which mauls their innards until their eyes are suffused with blood.

All this, comrades, our politicians are desperately far from understanding.

Even Comrade Moshe Dayan, who is a strong and wise young man, who is not lacking in cunning, still talks of Russia in geostrategic terms.

At least Moshe Dayan ought to be made immediately and sharply aware of the mounting danger.

Because time, ladies and gentlemen, time is running out.

Surely there is something sad and dark lurking behind all this, Russian expanses, Jewish depths, whirlpools of longing and hatred. For my part, many years ago I read a strange poem: a Russian symbolist, Vyacheslav Ivanov I think it was, wrote a restless sort of poem about polar bears yearning for palm trees in the desert, shifting sands under the blazing sun. Finally, in agony and longing, they are so consumed by savage melancholy that the saliva runs from their jaws. Na! In any case, comrades, I have talked too much. We must prepare for the worst. The primeval forces of nature, I say, cannot be warded off with diplomatics. It needs savagery. Cunning. Fury. We must bite again and again, furiously, desperately, like madmen, we must even use secret weapons, electrical and chemical devices, against our would-be murderers. Before it is too late. With your permission, I have finished. And I hereby invite the audience to ask questions.

Chapter six

The door was opened by a gentleman with a foreign expression, a gentleman in a suit and tie. He pressed himself against the wall of the corridor to let me pass and enter the room before him.

Inside, on the sofa, surrounded by cushions and pillows, reclined my Liuba. Without getting up, she extended her finger tips to me and said quietly:

'It must be Shraga. I wouldn't have recognized you in the street. It's been a long time, Shraga, since I saw you last. Sit down, Shraga. Hugo will go to the kitchen and make us three teas.'

The foreign gentleman, for his part, hurriedly put four short questions:

'Milk? Lemon? Sugar? Saccharin?'

Liuba said:

'Hugo, don't talk so much please. Perhaps instead of talking you wouldn't mind listening to me very carefully. Shraga sugar and lemon. Me as usual. You not a grain of sugar, Hugo. Now get going. Why are you standing there, staring like a calf? Just a minute. Wait, why are you running away, let me introduce you first: Shraga, this is Hugo, my new husband. You can see. A professor of graphology from Bucharest. Hugo, this is Comrade Shraga Unger. A big shot in the Party, and an intellectual to boot. Now what about the door. Would one of you mind closing it. Yes. Sit down, Shraga, sit down. Stop wandering round the room. Sit down. And don't look at me like that, any woman would lose her looks in this Tel Aviv air. What's the matter? You haven't got any prettier yourself over the years. So you're a fine one to talk. I told you, Shraga, sit down at last.'

I sat myself down and inspected the room. The room was full of vases, and the vases in turn were full of flowers. Even on the walls I could see pictures of flowers in vases.

So Liuba had held her own. She had not changed a bit.

And I was glad she had not changed. Most change is for the worse.

Meanwhile the foreign gentleman had come back with the tea. He also handed round cookies enthusiastically. He radiated frightened good manners. Between his mouth and his nose there emerged, as it were, a sort of yellow, sparse, snotty mustache. I cannot deny that I had had enough of this gentleman right from the start. More than enough.

Liuba said:

'Hugo is sorry, he has to go and water the plants on the balcony, so that I can chat with Shraga in private. I haven't seen Shraga in years. Hugo, the electric fan, please. No, not off. Did I tell you to turn it off? I asked you to move it. But why backwards, Hugo, why backwards when I want you to move it sideways?'

Hugo moved the fan sideways. Then he excused himself and went outside. I suddenly noticed that together with the suit and tie, the little man was wearing bedroom slippers. And I, for my part, revised my first opinion of Hugo on account of the bedroom slippers. A brown suit, a polka-dot tie, and bedroom slippers. What a pathetic combination.

Liuba said:

'So that's my husband, Shraga. You can see for yourself: another husband. You remember how every time I promised myself: enough weddings, Liuba, enough divorces. You've had enough. But if you think, Shraga, that I've got the strength to live on my own, I can't understand where you can have got hold of that idea. You're not God, Shraga. You can't understand everything. So don't set yourself up as a judge. You might start by taking a good look at yourself. That might stop you passing judgment on others. Never mind, Shraga, you can go on smoking. Smoke as much as you like. The air round here is thoroughly polluted anyway. Everywhere. Poisoned.'

Here I am, sitting talking to Liuba again, after all these years. And I won't deny that I feel a powerful sentiment welling up inside me. For my part, I've grown accustomed to loneliness. And now, suddenly a woman is talking to me again. Talking to me. And sending her own husband out of the room in my honor, as it were. How can I possibly contain my excitement? After all, it's Liuba: tall and gray, slightly angular, with a kind of grayish sparkle in her gray hair, her glance restless as ever, and only a touch of make-up.

And then, the sight of her fingers resting on her knees. And the sound of her voice again after all these years. Liuba.

I pulled the words together and said to her:

'Liuba, *krasavitsa*, time hasn't touched you. Still as charming as ever. You set my heart beating faster. And you're sweet, I must say, very sweet.'

Liuba raised her eyes and suddenly looked at me as though I had just come in.

'There you go, Shraga, always the flatterer. You always were free with your compliments. After all, I'm an old woman, Shraga, and you too, if it comes to that, you're an old man. This Tel Aviv is gradually getting the better of both of us. Of everyone who lives here. It's the old story. Are you surprised? Don't be. On the contrary. Let me ask you something, Shraga. What do we eat here all day, after all? Poisoned fruit. Poisoned vegetables. And what do we drink, Shraga? When you turn on the tap, what comes out? Answer me, what's the matter with you. Kindly answer me when I ask you a question. Well?'

'Cold water,' I said.

'That,' Liuba said, her eyes suddenly flashing, 'that's what *you* think. There's no more water left in Tel Aviv. You ought to know that. Finished. It's all a chemical solution. To kill the microbes, they pour hundreds of gallons, Shraga, hundreds of gallons of chemicals into the springs. Wait a minute, I haven't finished yet. And what about the air, Shraga? After all, you're something to do with the authorities. You're an important guy. You translate for them, you make speeches for them, so answer me this: What have you done to the air? The water? Nature in general? Why have you ruined everything all around us?'

'Liuba,' I tried to remonstrate, 'Liuba, you're not being quite fair. Are you short of air to breathe? Here we are, sitting together, chatting of this and that, and all the time we are filling our lungs with the good air of Israel. So what is it then that has suddenly made you so angry?'

'Carbon dioxide,' Liuba hissed venomously, 'it's all carbon dioxide. Foul gases. Acids. Filth. Gas. Diesel fumes. They burn thick smoke in Tel Aviv night and day. Look, Shraga, see with your own eyes how the trees are dying in every garden, in every avenue, all over the city thousands of trees are dying. Persian lilacs. Oleanders. Cypresses. Sycamores. If the trees could only cry out, Shraga, the whole city would shudder day and night. But trees are not like us. Trees die quietly. Without a murmur. They just stand there silently and stare and stare at us. In all the gardens, in all the avenues, in all the parks, in the squares, thousands of trees are dying without saying a word. And everywhere round about tons of soot. Chemical fumes. In our food. In our water. In our lungs and blood streams. Even the little babies aren't spared. Everything is being poisoned. Look at the piano, Shraga: even the white keys are turning black. Now excuse yourself and go out on the balcony for a moment. Tell Hugo I've sent you to see how the most delicate plants are going yellow. There's a smell of death, a smell of disaster all around, Shraga, I'm telling you. It was very kind of you to take the trouble to call. For years and years you and I appeared together on Friday nights in all sorts of settlements up and down the country, and suddenly years went by without our setting eyes on each other. You forgot me, Shraga. You forgot, and suddenly you remembered to come. Now you'll forget again. I'm not complaining, Shraga, after all, I forgot you almost completely too, and now in a flash I've remembered you. What sadness, Shraga, what sadness everywhere in everything. What's more, Shraga, you're very unhealthy. And you smoke too much.'

The foreign gentleman reappeared. This time he served little dishes of orange preserve, bowing slightly as he did so. He requested and received permission to sit. He even took advantage of a momentary lull in the conversation to express a vague criticism of the government.

Liuba, I learned, had for the last eleven years represented the Working Women's Council on the Commission for Clean Air.

In other words, this was her crusade.

If only we pooled our resources, she and I, we might be able to achieve something. We could support each other. I would sign the petition Liuba was about to launch on the authorities. I wouldn't refuse to sign. Why should I? In return, Liuba might agree to pull a string or two for me. Through Sashka, for instance, she could get in touch with Mulek, and Mulek could easily get hold of Moshe Dayan for me for an hour or two. More than that I wouldn't need. After all, in her day Liuba had several times sung for Ben Gurion himself.

So I got going and gave them a concise lecture. I spoke dramatically about the Bolshevik danger. About the thickening plot. Interstellar rockets. The conspiracy that was being hatched against the Jewish people. The destruction of the galaxy. Everything that was in my heart, concentrated and compressed into headings, as it were. All this had an exciting effect on Liuba's husband. Hugo several times interrupted my speech to interpose angry remarks about the younger generation.

Liuba silenced him.

And I too, for my part, stopped talking. A heavy black piano stood in the corner like a bad joke, covered with a scattering of ornaments. Elaborate figurines.

And the loneliness.

Her. Him. Me.

'Liuba,' I wanted to say, 'Mr. Hugo,' I wanted to say, 'why don't we decide to be brothers and sister. The three of us together. In other words, form a fraternity, a sort of commune. We'll all live together under one roof, share our bread, take it in turns to scrub the floor, take it in turns to put the garbage cans out, each of us free to talk to the others as much as he likes, whenever he likes, and to say whatever he likes. We'll never interrupt. We'll always listen to what our brother or sister is saying. We'll set up a kind of miniature kibbutz here. I'll go and get my collection of letters from Russian Jews. My newspaper clippings. My documents. My notes. And every evening I'll read aloud to you. Liuba, for her part, will play the piano for us. We'll even share Hugo's sorrow: he must have some spark, too.

'The heat is bound to die down. And then a wintry breeze will slowly start blowing off the sea. Winter itself is not too far off. And so the three of us will light the heater and sit here together through the long winter evenings. The samovar will be on the boil every evening until midnight. From time to time one of us will get up and pour tea for the others. We will be brothers. The windows, for their part, will be closed. We shall draw the curtains well at night, too, to keep out the sight of the wind and the water, and in this way we shall fortify ourselves against sadness. The heater will glow cheerfully. And none of us will be allowed to make fun of Hugo or hurt him. I'm sorry now, thoroughly sorry, for all the bad things I thought about Hugo earlier. I beg his pardon. I regret them and I take them back. I haven't had enough of him. After all, Hugo's face too bears the furrows of sorrow. And what of it, I ask myself, if one sorrow is not like another sorrow? Does that mean, I ask, that people cannot get close to one another? And I answer myself: That's nonsense. We must all definitely move closer. As close as possible. And use words to each other to the very limit of words. And try to touch each other occasionally, touch each other innocently.

'Is it not terrible, terrible and even ugly, humiliating, to live like this for years on end without touching anyone and without being touched?'

No, that's utterly absurd.

Could I really say something like that out loud? It would scare Liuba and Hugo out of their wits.

What a trite consolation. And compared with the silent expanse—how ridiculous it all is.

Liuba said: 'And what about the birds, Shraga. Even the birds. It's so terrible and frightening, the death of the birds. In another year or two there won't be a single bird left alive in the whole of Tel Aviv. Sometimes, Shraga, I stand here alone at my window as the evening comes on, and I can see the last birds desperately struggling to fly away. Perhaps they think they can escape. As if one could really escape from a poison that is already inside one. And so I stand quietly at the window, watching the sick birds fluttering from one dying tree to another. And then, Shraga, I am filled with a piercing sorrow, a desperate sorrow. And remorse. And longing too. Would crying help? And what loneliness I have, Shraga, what a loneliness, as if I had a child of my own and he was dying in front of my eyes.

'Do you remember what our Tel Aviv was like thirty, thirty-five years ago: a little town, a bright town, caressed by the breeze, with the tang of the sea in every room, the tang of the sea even in your sleep. The taste of the sunshine all day long, all summer long, and the meadows far away on the banks of the Yarkon, and the seedlings, the saplings among the newly built houses, and all those green gardens flourishing on the great sands. Caravans of quiet camels crossing the sands in the evening, their bells ringing in the distance. And before dawn hundreds of birds used to start singing in all the gardens round about. Even the construction workers used to sing all through the morning. Those young workers used to walk around half-naked, sun-tanned, bathed in sweat, on the scaffolding, endlessly singing those old songs. You can't have forgotten. They trundled heavy wheelbarrows up planks, and those songs came out so powerful and warm.

'And all those new avenues we had; the little trees that the children came down and watered with buckets. Why is it, Shraga, that everything is gradually being ruined? Why is the sea gray instead of blue? Why are the trees dying? Why is there soot and smoke everywhere? Such filth and stench all over the city. The rubbish, the noise, the new songs, and the ghastly cattle milling around in these horrible streets. Why, Shraga; what's it all in aid of? You tell me.

Please, Shraga, don't just sit there, say something. And all the pitch and fumes and tar. Tell me. Not you, Hugo, you keep your mouth shut, wait till we're talking about Bucharest. But you, Shraga, you remember as well as I do the loving there was here, the ideas, the narrow streets, the all-night arguments, the dashing young pioneers toiling with their own hands to pickle olives, the sandy lanes, the white houses with their tiled roofs, the little vegetable gardens, the birds, the flower nurseries, those delightful Friday literary evenings at Ohel Shem. And the sea, Shraga. What is this madness that has got the better of us and ruined everything. You have trampled Tel Aviv underfoot. The dreams, the ideals, the songs we used to sing. It's all dead, Shraga. And we should really have died too. It's all gone. Do you remember, Shraga, how pure the white sand was all around. The sky. The breeze. You're not laughing at me. Why aren't you laughing. Laugh, Shraga. Laugh like the rest of them. Like Ben Gurion, even, in the days when I used to stand and chat with him every Friday afternoon over his gate in Keren Kayemet Street. Go on, Shraga, laugh. I don't care. I couldn't care less. As far as I'm concerned, you can laugh, I don't mind.'

Hugo ventured to remark cautiously:

'And every day a new sensation. Me, I don't even buy any more the evening newspaper. All day mighty victories. Over the Suez Canal, over inflation, over the embargo, victories upon victories. It's all lies. No longer is it possible to know even what to believe and what not to believe. It's all sensation. I have even stopped listening now to Radio Cairo. They all cheat. This apart from what the lady says. I don't mean it against what the lady says. It is just my addition.'

'As for you, Hugo,' Liuba said, 'you shouldn't talk at all. They only got here yesterday, and already they're rambling on about everything under the sun. Back in Bucharest you spoke when you were spoken to. So why do you talk so much here. And once you start you never stop. Just you keep your mouth shut.'

'It's not the same,' Hugo said.

'It's exactly the same,' said Liuba.

Then Hugo got up and turned on the lights, because it was getting dark. As the light came on I saw Liuba close her eyes. My heart ached. And at that moment I felt a total despair. A clear, definite, almost mathematical despair. Each of us was on his own. Everyone is on his own.

And what a distance, I say, what a distance separates us all from each other. What dark distance, what galaxies of distance cut everyone off from everyone else. Listen, Comrade Hugo, you too, Liuba, we ought to get up all three of us this very minute and go and see Moshe Dayan in a body. Force him, that is, to listen to us. Na! It wouldn't hurt him to hear what we have to say. On the contrary, he ought to know once and for all how far things have gone. He ought to do something. Right away. Moshe Dayan should set our whole national machinery working without delay. At one fell stroke, and right now. This very night. Time is running out, running out.

There was nothing left to say. So I stood up and took my leave of Liuba and her husband. The foreign gentleman ran downstairs after me to hand me my cigarettes, which I had accidentally left on the coffee table. He was puffing and panting, and smiling his usual smile. We exchanged a kind of wave, at a distance, he at the top of the stairs and I at the bottom.

Well, why should I deny it, I had pinned some hopes on this visit to Liuba. Moreover, it had not been easy to find out her address, and I had hesitated uneasily before going to see her.

What hope? I asked myself.

Can such a question be answered in words?

I walked north alone along Ben Yehuda Street. Outside, night was falling. I was ill at ease. The city was so brightly lit and bustling. The evening was viciously humid. Below the city the sea crouched growling. A vapor rose from it and touched the whole city.

But the young people went on embracing in the streets as usual without apprehension.

And the cars hurried from place to place. A noisy tune came from the radio and permeated the whole of Tel Aviv. A little policeman sat at a pavement cafe wearing glasses, studying a magazine with apparently unusual seriousness. A large schoolboy eyed a passing girl's knees, and suddenly the girl herself glanced down at them. Another boy appeared and insisted on selling me an evening paper. I didn't refuse. Why should I.

The shopwindows hold a mirror to the street. A sort of pale orange halo hangs over the city. A solitary airplane groans complainingly overhead. Tiny lights alternate at its wing tips. What is in the pilot's heart it is not for me to know. He may be free from fear. After all, he, for his part, cannot know what is in my heart. Nothing but distance. There is a suppressed panting somewhere. The city is cheerful as usual. If this is calm, it is such a precarious calm that I myself am gradually filled with dread. And at the corner of Ben Yehuda Street and Arlosoroff Street I pronounce to myself the words:

Lost. All lost.

And indeed, objectively speaking, it is getting late.

Chapter seven

For many years I have been collecting newspaper clippings on a variety of subjects: Russian Jewry, Soviet politics and technology, the solar system, international communism, intrigues and upheavals in the Kremlin. I cut them out and stick them in albums. I also have a file where I keep dozens of private letters which have reached me in various ways from Russia.

I do not claim, of course, to be a researcher. I have no pretensions to being a systematic scholar. But I am entitled to claim that I have reached my own conclusions as a result of study and on the basis of facts that I have amassed. As for my perspective, I am subject to a slow, painful process of personal enlightenment.

It seems as though a logical contradiction intervenes between what I want to say and the words I use. But this contradiction, I maintain, is only apparent. In general, most contradictions are only apparent. Just like the planets in their orbits, the world of ideas tends toward circularity. And if even I myself have occasionally used expressions like 'the edge of the expanse,' I only fall into such cliches so as to express my depression.

For instance, some time ago I sat down by myself and studied *The History of Israeli Tank Warfare*. I read it page by page, chapter by chapter, from cover to cover. I didn't skip the maps, the photographs, not even the index.

As if I could understand the first thing about tank warfare. But, as I have already said, I am a curious man and I read a lot, and I am full of weird and wonderful ideas. In the midst of my thoughts I sometimes experience a sudden sensation.

There was one photograph with dozens of our tanks apparently rushing into battle in a great cloud of dust.

At the sight of this photograph I immediately felt a moment of inner awakening. My imagination started to picture this roaring Jewish onslaught appearing without warning at another time and somewhere completely different.

Imagine: not in Lower Galilee, not in the wilderness of Paran, but in the forests of Poland. Jewish armored columns suddenly start streaming furiously across the dark Polish forests. They shatter everything that stands in their way with bursts of savage fire: long Nazi convoys, trenches, bleak fortifications. A hurricane of destruction is unleashed on Poland and no force in the world can stop it. An armored Jewish maelstrom sweeps across the Slavic landscape, devastating forests and fields, thundering on and on and on.

This image, I cannot deny, aroused a surging excitement inside me which I have not experienced for years. Can you possibly share this grim fantasy with me: hundreds of furious Jewish tanks crossing the length and breadth of Poland, brutally trampling our murderers underfoot, inscribing a savage Hebrew message across the scorched earth with their tracks in letters of fire and smoke. And at daybreak, in a lightning attack, forcing their way into the outskirts of a terrified Warsaw. The last remaining German troops scattering for their lives in every direction, the fists of fury herding them though street after street, alley after alley. A trembling, shivering Warsaw peers out from behind barred shutters.

Then the cascades of fire suddenly burst into the beleaguered Ghetto. At the thunder of the tanks the last Jewish defenders, desperate exhausted boys, merge dazed from crannies and sewers, clutching their pathetic weapons, and press themselves against the wall with wide-staring eyes.

For an instant an otherworldly silence descends on the scene. Nothing stirs.

And a moment later, in an outburst of mad joy, shouting, welling tears, the Jews of the Ghetto clasp the tanks to their breasts. With delirious fingers they explore the Jewish steel. What savage rejoicing. It is as if the heavens have opened and the vengeance of the martyrs has hurtled to earth with horrific rage. The remnants of the Gestapo flee, convulsed by panic, trampled left and right by merciless tracks of steel. And the guns calmly and systematically smash the last remaining nests of murderers.

Can the heart contain it?

My thirst still rages unquenched.

Then with lightning speed my tanks turn and thunder eastward. It's coming, it's coming, it's here. With furious wrath they hound all the bands of butchers of the Jews: Poles, Lithuanians, Ukrainians. In a single panting rush. Without a break. Without looking back to see what is burned and what is crushed. Eastward. The vast fields of snow are torn to shreds. A mighty whip-blow over the length and breadth of all the cursed Slavic lands.

And from all the villages, hundreds of blasted villages lost in the snowy wilderness, peasants run to seek the shelter of the forests. They run for their lives, as if the Devil himself were at their heels. And I can see Jews in their thousands lining all the routes. Gladness wells up and stifles them. They bite their lips with excitement. The joy is almost more than flesh and blood can bear. While from the turrets of the tanks our own boys wave back. They too are moved; the shadow of their helmets may conceal a tear.

I can see the land trembling. I can see the vast snowy plains stretching out in silent submission to those hooves of steel. The rage of the Jews all over the land. Defeated Red armies, fragments of shattered divisions, wandering among the swamps in search of a hiding place. Forests upon forests ablaze with fire. Even the snow seems caught in the flames. The terror of the peasants. Village churches totter and collapse. Loved-hated cities open wide their gates. Vilna. Kovno. Bialystok. The whole of Russia is falling, town after town. Fierce Jewish rage, savagely unleashed, foams up and bursts its bounds. The foeland crumbles to dust piece by piece. And I, from the bottom of my soul, I whisper in the language of my forefathers: Amen, amen.

I can see the low gray sky. Endless snow on the steppes. And the galloping tanks move onward, ever onward. From Minsk to Smolensk the Russian soil shudders and groans. One after another the Red armies are routed. The Supreme Soviet itself breaks up in disorder and flees eastward to hide beyond the Urals until the trouble has passed. And under rotting wooden crosses generations of Jew-killers turn impotently in their graves. The whole of Russia is writhing, writhing in panic, writhing with the screams of desperate women. A blind, white-hot anger is piercing her flesh like a knife to the very depths of the plains and drives everything to submission. Kiev, Kharkov, the Dnieper basin, Rostov-on-Don. Everything is devastated. The vengeance of the Jews is erupting.

Kishinev. All around the main square masses of huge-boned Russians are assembled, their hands raised high, a fawning smile on their faces. A procession of Orthodox priests emerges from the darkness of the church carrying tall crosses and chanting an ancient hymn. And on the other side of the square my own Russian Jewry stand watching in silence.

And I can see Moshe Dayan, in his dusty battle-dress, standing awesome and gaunt as he receives in a grim silence the surrender of the Governor-General of Kishinev.

All the church bells ring out. On the plains herds of horses rear up on their hind legs. The fury of the Jews sweeps on and on.

My heart inside me, like a wild thing, bursts into savage howls. But after a while there came a limpness.

I took another look at the photograph and said to myself:

Tanks. Na! Such clumsy machines. And for the time being all we are facing is miserable Arabs.

And can I gain any relief from a book on tank warfare?

How absurd it all is.

So I sat down and wrote a long letter to the divorcee next door. For a whole morning I formulated, crossed out, and polished. I wanted her permission to send for a plumber. Our party wall, the wall which divides us, that is, is rotting with damp. A water pipe seems to have become corroded, and the wetness is spreading. It has been going on for several years now, and how long can one suffer in silence. If something is not done about it, the whole building may disintegrate. And in order to replace the old pipe with a new one, it will be necessary to demolish the whole wall and rebuild it afresh afterward. I hereby undertake responsibility for all the expenses, I am not here concerned with financial questions, but merely desire her consent. That is the reason I have taken the liberty of troubling her, et cetera.

Of course, I could simply have rung her doorbell. Or I could at least have bent down and pushed the letter under her door on my way out. But no, I sent my letter through the post, properly stamped, and it was through the post that I received her reply: she was planning to move to another area in a few weeks' time, and she would appreciate it if I would be kind enough to wait for the new tenants to move in, and address any complaints to them and not to her.

So what was the point, I ask, of the whole exercise. None whatever.

On the contrary: disappointment. I was sorry she was leaving. I was grateful to her and her former husband. Once, in the year '59, I fainted slightly on the stairs. Apparently I was knocked out by fatigue. The ex-husband came out and picked me up, and supported me on his shoulder. He was going to help me to my apartment, but at the last minute she came out and said to him, 'Issachar, you might as well bring him in here.' They took me into their apartment and laid me down gently on the sofa in the living room. The man Issachar placed a towel soaked in cold water on my forehead while the lady made coffee. When I came to I was deeply grateful to them. Only, in my usual way, I exaggerated my thanks to the point of embarrassing them. Despite this embarrassment, the husband did not omit to say to me as I was leaving: 'Look in and see us sometime, Mr. Unger; we can have a cup of coffee and a neighborly chat.' And his wife, for her part, added: 'It could happen to any of us. Neighbors should help each other. Don't mention it, Mr. Unger, think nothing of it. Remember to come and see us.'

I weighed up this invitation in my mind for some time, but a few months later they started shouting on the other side of the wall. And after that they apparently decided to divorce and go their separate ways. And how, I ask, could I visit a woman who lives on her own. Moreover, not long afterward the lover began to make his appearance and to stay all night, which confirmed certain suspicions of mine. And now here she is moving out to another area. It's all over. Have I perhaps missed something? Na! What a ridiculous idea.

Meanwhile I composed and sent a personal letter to Hugo. Comrade Hugo, I wrote, it has not escaped my notice that you are a lonely man. I have no good news to offer you. Only I should like you to know that you are by no means alone in the world. In the first place, from now on I take the liberty of considering you as a friend. With your permission, of course. Secondly, spare a thought for the flavor of the nights here in Tel Aviv, in summer or even in winter. There is no other city in the whole world, Hugo, where so many people dream such terrible dreams every night. In other words, the mathematical proportion between the population and the total amount of suffering is enormous. Shocking. Just sit down at night, if you please, alone on the balcony. Wrap up well on account of the dew, and sit on the balcony until dawn. You will surely hear, through the open bedroom windows, how this whole Jewish city cries out in its sleep. It is the sound of nightmares, Hugo, of horrors past and horrors yet to come, all compressed on these hot dry nights. We are granted no more than a brief breathing space. A precarious, ephemeral respite. A short reprieve. The Jewish people, Hugo, are totally unable to withdraw from the game once and for all. Did we really hope to take refuge here and build a new land and pretend to be a Bulgaria or a New Zealand? Think it over, Hugo: Are we really capable of sitting here quietly for the next thousand years, plowing all day or buying and selling horses, drinking in taverns or dancing with peasant girls in the evening, sleeping peacefully all night long, and then getting up and repeating the whole routine the next day? Are we capable of suddenly becoming a nation of heavy, hardheaded, sleepy, belching peasants? Na! It would be utter nonsense even to entertain such an idea. I turn to you as a close friend. I want to open your eyes. Let me tell you something, Hugo: All the anger, all the misery, all the enthusiasm, all the hysteria, all the madness in the world, all the revolutions and ideologies and complexes and suffering and horror, everywhere, are all directed against us.

So it has been in every generation gone by, and so it will be in every generation to come. There is a terrible passion, Hugo, a mad, murderous passion in the heart of every people and at the root of every ideology. I for one do not know the name of this sinister passion. But I do know that it is directed against us day and night, threatening us, radiating toward us all the time. Even here. Even on the balcony facing the sea in Tel Aviv.

What terror, Hugo. What blind panic.

And is Israel, I ask, an invincible fortress? Is it a God-forsaken island in the middle of the ocean?

No, Hugo. That's a mistake. A total mistake.

Let's take a look at Israel together. A narrow strip stretching between the arching sea and the vast deserts. Look, Hugo, see what this narrow strip contains. A few flocks of white houses strung out here and there. A few citrus groves, telegraph poles, metal signposts along the wayside, bearing names of new settlements A few water pipes branching hither and thither. Asphalt roads. Brightly painted motor coaches moving from place to place. A few tender plantations of saplings. Some vegetable gardens. Wet paint. New housing projects, prefabricated or built of concrete blocks. Patches of lawn. Tiled roofs. Dogs barking madly. You see, Hugo, it's all unstable, impermanent, almost pathetic. Admittedly it's attractive and endearing. Don't get me wrong, Hugo: I love these basking, wind-swept, sun-washed settlements with all my heart and soul. I, too, in my own way, share in the love and hopes. Passionately. But a cold shiver suddenly creeps down my spine: What's going to happen here, Hugo? Where is it all leading? What is in store, what is it that is stirring in the dark?

And time, Hugo, time.

I say to myself: If only the Jewish people had a gigantic rocket, a terrifying monster of hitherto unknown dimensions, then Moshe Dayan could suddenly stand up and declare to all the nations: Ladies and gentlemen, do not dare, please. Do not touch. If you have fingers, we have fists. If you have knives, we have a terrible stratagem. Henceforth if anyone tries to harm us we will go mad and blow up the whole planet. We have our secret rays. If you dare to attack, we may turn our rays on Neptune or Jupiter, divert it from its orbit, bring it down on top of your heads and send the slivers flying to the farthest ends of the galaxy. Na!

On the other hand, we could concoct another plan. We could devise and construct a mechanical device by means of which we could all, all the Jewish people both young and old, leave and emigrate together to some faraway planet in another galaxy. And there, Hugo, far off in the depths of the silent expanse, beyond the reach of any power, we may rebuild a kind of heavenly Jerusalem. And so, Hugo, we will find rest. At long last we will be surrounded only by the simplest and most powerful elements. Water. Wind. Light. Silence. We shall know peace. Peace, Hugo, perfect, final peace.

And maybe even love.

Here ended my letter to Hugo. To Hugo, not to Liuba, though no doubt it would fall into her hands too. If indeed I made up my mind to post it.

Meanwhile a minor disaster occurred in Tel Aviv: Huma Spielberg, the Health Service nurse, who used to give me my injections twice a week, suddenly passed away one fine day.

On Tuesday morning I went to the Zamenhof Clinic as usual, and there was no Huma Spielberg. Nor would there be. From now on who will give me the injections I need? Some little trainee nurse, some undersized pallid Iraqi girl. Will she be able to hide her disgust at my thick old body, and my language. The jokes I come out with. My bad breath. After all, I feel disgust myself.

A Soviet fleet has suddenly appeared at Port Said and Latakia, so I learned this morning from the headlines in the newspaper. The editorial believes we are in for another round of psychological warfare. And what about Moshe Dayan? He is laughing, laughing right across the front page, laughing in a collar and tie, surrounded by throngs of merry entertainers at some gala concert.

Comrade Dayan, I say, if you will only be good enough to take a look over your shoulder, you will see generations upon generations of Jews watching you, and all of them, if you don't mind, in deadly earnest. The whole world is holding its breath and waiting. And you, meanwhile, you permit yourself to stand about like that, laughing aloud and slapping some nobody on the back.

Imagine. Suddenly I walk in, alone. I stand on my own in the dark at the back of the auditorium. I can see you but you can't see me.

I send you an urgent note by one of the ushers. Three lines in my frantic handwriting. You read it and then read it again. Your expression clouds over. At once you purse your lips and exchange whispers with your confidential aide. You slip out in the middle of a movement, by a side entrance. I can see you going down the stairs, with a measured, sinuous tread. Unhurriedly you stoop and get into the driver's seat. You tear off your jacket and tie and toss them into the back seat. And now you are driving quickly and expertly through the busy streets. Your breathing is regular. Your hands on the wheel are relaxed. Your face is alternately lit up and darkened in the flashing light of the neon signs. A calm inner rhythm guides your far-ranging thoughts. Swiftly they focus on the central issue. All the possible lines converge on a single crucial point.

Decision.

Round your mouth I can see the lines of silent determination.

This way or that.

This way.

And so finally I arrive at the bottommost depths of my thoughts. Everything depends then on my ability to compose this urgent note. To concentrate everything into three lines. I need a powerful spark. Words. One short note that will bring illumination to the Minister of Defense.

That will be the culmination of my mission. Then I shall

experience relief. I shall be free to rest, or to shut myself up and live in pure meditation. Perhaps to die. All I have to do is to put three lines on paper, and send them up to the platform by an usher.

Only, I ask, what words can one use? So I am back again where I began: words.

Are there any possible words?

Na! I have more or less miserably failed.

I must hold my peace.

Only this:

I am gradually coming to terms with the idea of giving up. I must accept a compromise. How distasteful I suddenly find this obstinacy of my old age. There is an inaudible line up to which words may reach and beyond which there begins the expanse of silence. I can see this abstract line now as if it were here before me. The man who would dare to cross it must be completely out of his mind.

I must hold my peace.

First thing tomorrow I shall go to the Cultural Bureau. I shall walk in cheerfully, swallowing my bitterness, and I shall calmly announce: I agree. Na! I accept. These long drives late at night are not good for me. It is time for me to take a rest. And it is true that the style I employ in my lectures, that rumbustious style of mine, cursing the Bolsheviks and so on, does not suit these changing times. I'm through. Change the guard, then, as you see fit. I hereby accept the post of stylistic editor. No more crazy drives from kibbutz to kibbutz along deserted roads on Friday nights. I've had enough. From now on I'll stay here. I'll spend my days translating on demand. To the best of my modest abilities.

But I have one request to make, comrades. Call it a whim if you like, but it's an earnest plea. I'd like to have a little office of my own, with just a desk and a chair, here in the Central Committee Building, and specifically on one of the upper floors. I want to be able to glance up from my work occasionally and look out at the sea. And so the sea breeze can reach me through the open window. It's not an unreasonable request.

And under my breath I shall add:

I'll buy a pair of powerful binoculars.

When no one is looking I shall scan the horizon. I shall always be on guard. For as long as the reprieve lasts I shall participate fully. Just like everyone else. But when the gray ships appear over the distant horizon, I shall be the first to raise the alarm. I shall raise the alarm with all my dwindling strength, raise it with my dying gasp. With the last gasp of my love.

After all, it is only out of love that I—

And here is the brink of silence.

1970

About the Author

Amos Oz

Amos Oz was born in 1939 in Jerusalem, and at the age of fifteen went to live on Kibbutz Hulda. He studied philosophy and literature at the Hebrew University of Jerusalem, and has been a visiting fellow at Oxford University, Hebrew University and Colorado College. He has been named Officer of Arts and Letters of France. An author of prose for both children and adults, as well as an essayist, he has been widely translated and is internationally acclaimed. He lives in the south, in Arad, and teaches literature at Ben Gurion University in the Negev.

The fonts used in this book are from the Garamond family

Other works by Amos Oz
are available from *The* Toby Press

Soumchi

The Toby Press publishes fine writing,
available at bookstores everywhere. For more information,
please contact *The* Toby Press at www.tobypress.com